Seneca: *Hercules Furens*

COMPANIONS TO GREEK AND ROMAN TRAGEDY

Series Editor: Thomas Harrison

Seneca: *Hercules Furens*

Neil W. Bernstein

BLOOMSBURY ACADEMIC
LONDON • NEW YORK • OXFORD • NEW DELHI • SYDNEY

BLOOMSBURY ACADEMIC
Bloomsbury Publishing Plc
50 Bedford Square, London, WC1B 3DP, UK
1385 Broadway, New York, NY 10018, USA

BLOOMSBURY, BLOOMSBURY ACADEMIC and the Diana logo are
trademarks of Bloomsbury Publishing Plc

First published in Great Britain 2017
Paperback edition first published 2018

A catalogue record for this book is available from the British Library.

Library of Congress Cataloging-in-Publication Data
Names: Bernstein, Neil W., 1973- author.
Title: Seneca, Hercules furens / Neil W. Bernstein.
Other titles: Companions to Greek and Roman tragedy.
Description: London ; New York : Bloomsbury Academic, 2017. |
Series: Companions to Greek and Roman tragedy
Identifiers: LCCN 2016048851| ISBN 9781474254922 (hb) |
ISBN 9781474254915 (epdf)
Subjects: LCSH: Seneca, Lucius Annaeus, approximately 4 B.C–65 A.D.
Hercules furens.
Classification: LCC PA6664.H43 B47 2017 | DDC 872/.01–dc23 LC record
available at https://lccn.loc.gov/2016048851

ISBN: HB: 978-1-4742-5492-2
PB: 978-1-3500-8081-2
ePDF: 978-1-4742-5491-5
ePub: 978-1-4742-5493-9

Series: Companions to Greek and Roman Tragedy

Typeset by RefineCatch Limited, Bungay, Suffolk

To find out more about our authors and books visit
www.bloomsbury.com and sign up for our newsletters.

Leonard and Danielle Bernstein, parentibus optimis

Yi-Ting Wang, Hannah Wang Bernstein, and Isabelle Miranda Wang Bernstein,
uxori filiabusque carissimis

κωφὸς ἀνήρ τις, ὃς Ἡρακλεῖ στόμα μὴ περιβάλλει.
Any man is dumb who does not embrace Heracles with his speech.
Pindar, Pythia 9.87 (tr. Race)

Contents

List of Illustrations

Acknowledgments

ὅστις δὲ πλοῦτον ἢ σθένος μᾶλλον φίλων / ἀγαθῶν πεπᾶσθαι βούλεται, κακῶς φρονεῖ. I am grateful to the many friends who have contributed to the creation of this book. Tom Carpenter, Neil Coffee, Matt Cornish, Andrew Escobedo, Kyle Gervais, Micaela Janan, Leo Landrey, Lauren Donovan Ginsberg, Bill Owens, Rachel Thomas, Chris Trinacty, Wheaton Wood, Yi-Ting Wang, and the two anonymous readers all read the manuscript in full or part and offered many helpful suggestions. John Farmanesh-Bocca generously took time from a busy performance and direction schedule to describe in detail the process of bringing *Hercules Furens* to the stage. No one named here is responsible for the errors and infelicities that remain in this book, which are exclusively my own.

I am grateful to Tom Harrison and Alice Wright for commissioning this book for the Bloomsbury Companions to Greek and Roman Tragedy Series. Todd Bastin invited me to give a series of lectures on Seneca's tragedies at the Athens, Ohio Public Library. Dr. Wheaton Wood offered a professional psychiatrist's insights on psychotic episodes. Isabelle Bernstein watched Disney's *Hercules* many more times than I did and pointed out several details that I missed. I thank Mónica P. Martín Díaz and the Museo Arqueológico Nacional (Madrid, Spain) for permission to reproduce the calyx krater by Asteas. Jones Welsh kindly provided permission to reproduce images from Not Man Apart Physical Theatre Company's production of *Hercules Furens*. Kim Fisher offered timely help in the preparation of the index. The College of Arts and Sciences and the Department of Classics and World Religions at Ohio University provided financial support for the purchase of image rights.

My family, my true heroes, have once more encouraged and supported another book. As always, my greatest thanks are due to them.

Preface

What is the worst misfortune that could strike the world's greatest hero in his moment of ultimate triumph? How does viewing his suffering affect traditional ideas of heroism? Does true heroism consist in slaying monsters and overthrowing tyrants, or in enduring misfortunes and acknowledging responsibilities to others? These are some of the major questions posed by Seneca in his tragedy *Hercules Furens*, which he composed in the middle of the first century CE. Hercules returns from his greatest Labor, the kidnapping of the monster Cerberus from the Underworld, just in time to save his family from being killed by the usurping tyrant Lycus. Immediately after that, the Fury (sent by the vengeful goddess Juno) drives the hero temporarily insane and causes him to murder his wife and children. Juno drives Hercules to kill his loved ones, yet the hero immediately accepts responsibility for his actions once he returns to his senses. Hercules then faces an ethical conflict: whether he should escape his guilt through heroic suicide or heed the pleas of his father and his friend Theseus to live on. In narrating this tragic reversal and its aftermath, Seneca explores the meanings of ambition, madness, and responsibility.

This book may have a Herculean subject, but not a Herculean scale. Its ambitions are modest: it seeks to introduce Seneca's *Hercules Furens* to undergraduates and general readers who have not yet studied the Latin language or Roman culture. There has been a resurgence of popular interest in Seneca in the twenty-first century. His multiple roles as ambitious courtier, imperial tutor, public intellectual, and would-be moralist compromised by his closeness to power have fascinated every generation since Nero's reign. In the last generation, three major biographies of Seneca written for general readers have appeared in English.[1] This book sets *Hercules Furens* in the contexts of Greco-Roman literary tradition, Seneca's varied career and prolific writings, and the reception of Senecan tragedy from antiquity to the present decade.

Chapter 1, "Introducing *Hercules Furens*," briefly summarizes the action of the play and the themes that the subsequent chapters discuss in greater detail. The summaries alternate with discussions of aspects of Roman culture and stagecraft that are likely unfamiliar to modern theatergoers. Seneca's characters have very different moral assumptions from our own. For example, the Chorus's combination of misogyny, class prejudice, and disdain for urban life likely appears repugnant to a modern audience. Yet they are exactly what an audience of Roman aristocrats would have expected based on literary tradition and conventional assumptions. The chapter also discusses the purposes of the play's speeches (in part because their length is often off-putting to modern audiences), the different connotations of their generic forms, and their numerous allusions to classical mythology.

Chapter 2, "Major Themes in *Hercules Furens*," discusses the play's exploration of the themes of madness, courage, suicide, ancestry, and landscape. The question of Hercules' responsibility has been a major line of division in modern criticism of the play. My reading does not discount Hercules' present guilt nor his past history of violence; it rather calls attention to the literary tradition of Juno's instigation. Setting aside the murder of his family, Hercules' restless, self-aggrandizing ambition inevitably conflicts with contemporary views of heroes as modest, self-sacrificing, and other-directed. Studying the Latin word *virtus*, whose primary meanings are "manliness, courage, machismo," helps in understanding the difference between Seneca's Hercules and contemporary heroes. Where contemporary understanding typically relates suicide to mental illness, the Roman aristocracy could also perceive the act as one of the consummate expressions of manly courage (*virtus*).

Much of *Hercules Furens* Act 5 concerns the efforts of Amphitryon and Theseus to persuade Hercules that his obligations to his father and friend supersede his obligation to expiate his guilt. This scene confirms the depth of the love that Hercules and Amphitryon feel for one another. The fact that Amphitryon loves a son that he knows is not his own is one of several examples in the play of a changed attitude toward the connection between ancestry and identity. Juno persecutes Hercules because of his identity as Jupiter's illegitimate son, while the humbly born Lycus sees no bar to usurping the throne of Thebes and praises himself as a self-made man. Seneca wrote for audiences who had wealth and social power but not necessarily distinguished ancestry, and throughout his writings he reevaluates the traditional meaning of ancestry. The chapter concludes with an examination of the play's moralized landscapes, including the city and the country, Thebes and Athens, and Scythia and the Underworld. Description of landscape forms a major component of the characters' speeches in *Hercules Furens*, and the contrast between the characters' perceptions of landscape creates dramatic conflict.

Chapter 3, "Monster-slayer, Moral Exemplar, and Madman: Hercules' Ancient Roles," discusses the Greco-Roman literary and artistic traditions that inform the play. Seneca isolated particular themes from a lengthy and varied tradition of representing Hercules' madness. In Euripides' *Heracles*, the only other extant tragedy about Hercules' madness, the personification of madness (Lussa) appears on stage to drive the hero mad. Seneca's audience, by contrast, must infer from Hercules' madness that Juno has succeeded in her planned revenge. Euripides' influential version of the story contributed to a widespread tradition of the maddened Hercules, found in contexts as varied as artworks, medical texts, and comic parodies of tragedy. Seneca's educated viewers also knew Virgil's *Aeneid* and Ovid's *Metamorphoses* in detail, as they were the literary classics of the preceding generation and an integral part of their cultural education.

Seneca evokes both poems from the first line of *Hercules Furens*. Virgil's Hercules, as hero of *virtus*, serves as a foil for Aeneas, the hero of duty. Seneca also reprises the narrative pattern found through the *Metamorphoses'* Theban stories, in which Juno destroys innocent victims connected to Jupiter's illegitimate children. The vengeful goddess of *Hercules Furens* appears in a tragic Thebes that directly recalls Ovid's influential representation of the mythical city. In every scene, Seneca invites comparison with the mythical characters and settings of the Augustan epics.

Chapter 4, "*Hercules Furens* and Seneca's Career," sets the tragedy in the context of the playwright's roles as a Neronian courtier and a prolific author of tragedies and essays on Stoic philosophy. Seneca's satire *Apocolocyntosis* ("Pumpkinification") mocking the recently deceased emperor Claudius appears to parody *Hercules Furens*. On the basis of this connection, scholars speculatively date the tragedy to sometime before late 54 CE. The chapter then traces some of the intersections between the themes of *Hercules Furens* and those of Seneca's other tragedies and his philosophical essays. One of Seneca's greatest legacies to subsequent Western theater was the figure of the revenger who stops at nothing to see his or her enemy defeated, and who imagines some act of violence greater than what other revengers have yet achieved. Seneca uses his audience's knowledge of literary tradition to create a metatheatrical dimension in each of his tragedies. Hercules argues that passive acceptance of defeat means he would not be Hercules, and that committing suicide would be his thirteenth and greatest Labor. The self in Senecan tragedy is not given or immutable, but rather a rhetorical assessment of the degree of coincidence between actual behavior and the expectations created by tradition.

Philosophers long before Seneca used Hercules as a traditional character in spiritual allegories. They appealed to his labors and his apotheosis as a means of discussing wise people's goal of preserving high ethical standards as they struggle with life's challenges. The

Chorus of *Hercules Furens* praises many of the choices that ordinary people make in the name of ethical improvement, but it is clear that they do not apply to the extraordinary hero. As the Chorus and his own family repeatedly ask, what good are Hercules' deeds if they bring him no personal benefit and leave his family insecure? The philosophical essays make Hercules a good figure to think with by focusing on the contrast between his pursuit of worldly success and the Stoic's pursuit of self-improvement. Seneca's philosophical writings often praise endurance as the truly heroic aspect of the wise person's character. No matter how much weaker the wise person's body may be than Hercules', he or she nevertheless endures through life's challenges with moral integrity. Despair threatens to consume Hercules at the end of his tragedy, but wise people know better than to succumb.

Chapter 5, "Performance and Reception," examines the adaptation of *Hercules Furens* from antiquity to the present in a variety of media. The chapter begins by examining the ongoing debates among scholars over performance of the plays in Seneca's day, then traces the reception of *Hercules Furens* into the present decade. It would be impossible to imagine Renaissance theater without Seneca's contribution. Slaney catalogs the properties that made Senecan tragedy attractive to Renaissance dramatists: "rhetoric, excess, metatheatricality, delirium, possession, abjection, horror, confinement, or *sympatheia* [responsiveness between protagonists and their surrounding environment]."[2] The tragedies of Shakespeare and his contemporary Marlowe are used as examples of the tremendous influence of *Hercules Furens*. The figure of Hercules functions as a pagan contrast in Shakespeare's exploration of the guilt of characters such as Lear and Macbeth, who cannot blame their deeds on divine agents.

Seneca's fortunes declined after the Renaissance, as critics and audiences objected to his non-naturalistic characterization and the lengthy speeches that do not appear to advance the dramatic action. Yet the central image of *Hercules Furens*, the hero who follows his victory over death by murdering his own family, continues to trouble and fascinate audiences two thousand years after Seneca's version. A 2011 production of *Hercules Furens* at the Getty Villa in Malibu, California, written and directed by John Farmanesh-Bocca, explores the interpretation of Hercules as a victim of combat trauma. Popular film shows a greater discomfort with representing Hercules' madness and family violence. As might be expected in a story aimed at young children, the Disney cartoon *Hercules* (1997) celebrates traditional family values. The Paramount/MGM *Hercules* (2014) begins after the hero's putative murder of the family, but makes some characteristic narrative compromises in order to avoid a negative view of its hero. The film deviates from the darker narrative of its source material, Moore and Wijaya's graphic novel *Hercules: The Thracian Wars* (2008). *Thracian Wars* acknowledges Hercules' responsibility for the murder of his family and represents him and his band of mercenaries as warriors for life, unable to live among civilians. On this view, Hercules' return from the Underworld models the veteran's difficulty in reintegrating into a peacetime community. However anachronistic Seneca might have found this interpretation, it demonstrates that *Hercules Furens* still addresses modern audiences' contemporary concerns—the task that we have always called upon classical texts to perform.

The book concludes with a Chronology, Glossary of Greek and Latin Terms, and annotated Bibliography with suggestions for Further Reading. All Greek and Latin has been translated. Unless indicated otherwise, all translations of Seneca's tragedies are taken from Wilson, *Seneca: Six Tragedies* (Oxford, 2010). Line numbers refer to Wilson's numeration. Translations of Seneca's philosophical works are taken from Asmis, Bartsch, and Nussbaum, eds, *The Complete Works of Lucius Annaeus Seneca* (Chicago, 2010–). Translations of works not yet included in this series and other classical works are taken from Loeb Classical Library editions unless otherwise indicated.

1

Introducing *Hercules Furens*

Act 1, lines 1–124

The goddess Juno, sister and wife of Jupiter, the king of the gods, appears alone on stage before dawn. Her furious monologue comprises the play's first act, and represents the only appearance by a god or goddess in Senecan tragedy. She describes various constellations in the night sky who were once her husband Jupiter's rape victims and illegitimate children, transformed into stars after their deaths (1–18). Hercules, Jupiter's son by Alcmene, causes Juno particular anxiety and frustration. She worries that he will ascend to heaven in his father's place and that his mother Alcmene will take her place as queen of heaven. Juno has accordingly attempted to destroy Hercules by compelling him to perform twelve difficult and dangerous Labors. Some of the Labors involved killing monsters such as the Nemean Lion, the Hydra, and the birds of the Stymphalian swamp. Other Labors required him to travel to distant locations, such as to western Iberia to kill the three-bodied monster Geryon, and to Scythia to seize the belt of Hippolyte, the queen of the Amazons. Instead of dying, however, Hercules has triumphed over each challenge and so proved his divine parentage.

As the action of the play is beginning, Hercules has just completed his final Labor, bringing the three-headed monster Cerberus up from the Underworld (19–63). Now that he has returned alive from the Underworld, Juno worries that he intends to make an assault on heaven, depose his father Jupiter, and make himself king of the gods.

She contemplates sending Jupiter's traditional enemies, the Titans and Typhoeus, against Hercules, but remembers that he earlier helped Jupiter defeat them as well (63–83). Juno realizes that the only adversary who can oppose Hercules is himself. She resolves to summon the demonic Furies from the Underworld to drive Hercules mad, along with other allegorical figures such as the personifications of Crime and Madness. The angry goddess threatens to stand beside Hercules and guide his weapons as he murders his family in a maddened frenzy (84–122). Her speech concludes with an announcement of the dawning day (123–4).

Juno's lengthy tirade characterizes her not as an authoritative, sublimely distant queen of the gods, but as excessively angry, fearful, and vindictive. The aggrieved wife's anger at Jupiter's adulteries may be justified, but she directs her anger not against her husband but against his innocent rape victims and their children. Such blaming of the victims is common in stories of illegitimacy from Greek mythology, but Juno goes beyond this already unjust norm. The indication of excessiveness in her rage begins as early as line 12, when she complains about sharing the sky with Orion. Orion does not belong on the list of descendants of Jupiter's numerous adulteries, nor was Ariadne ever one of Jupiter's rape victims (18). Before she has even mentioned Hercules, then, Juno has attempted moral policing of the constellations. Her fear that Hercules will storm heaven and depose his father Jupiter (63–74) is similarly overblown. If Hercules were indeed so powerful, he could have repulsed Juno's earlier assaults, ignored the command to perform the Labors, and undertaken the conquest of heaven. Juno's tirade accordingly reveals more about her paranoia and jealousy than it does about Hercules and his supposed threats.

Beginning the play with a speech by an angry, jealous Juno would guide a Roman audience to think of Virgil's *Aeneid*. Virgil's Juno tries to destroy Aeneas first with a storm and next with a war, and similarly finds that her efforts are ineffective. Just as Hercules triumphs through successful completion of the Labors, so Aeneas triumphs over the adversities that Juno sends. Seneca's Juno instead chooses a more insidious means of assault. She will send the Furies to drive Hercules mad, and thus direct the hero's own unconquerable strength against himself and his loved ones. This form of revenge recalls the vindictive Juno of Ovid's *Metamorphoses*, a character inspired by Virgil's Juno, who maddens the Theban king Athamas and causes him to kill his own child. The Roman audience of Juno's extended monologue would have accordingly understood her speech as a sophisticated response to earlier angry Juno characters.

First Chorus, lines 125–204

The Chorus enter the stage and describe the dawning day. In the Latin script, they enter the stage singing in an anapaestic meter, a rhythm composed of two light beats and one heavy beat typically used in marching songs.[1] (As with every other detail of the stage performance of Seneca's tragedies, however, the text provides no information regarding the stage movement or dancing that accompanied this rhythm.) The stars disappear in the morning light and the birds begin to sing. The Chorus then describe how rural people in various occupations (farming, sailing, and fishing) turn to their work as the day begins (125–58). They then contrast this picture of secure and peaceful rural life with the anxieties and moral pitfalls of city life. A series of urban figures represents the vices of the city: the dependent client who must seek support from powerful patrons, the avaricious man who is perpetually unsatisfied with his gains, the politician beholden to the fickle mob, and the lawyer who sells his skills at argument (159–74). In the Chorus' view, Hercules has made a worse error than the ambitious but deluded city dwellers. Rather than being content with the short lifetime that human beings are allotted by fate, he has chosen to speed on his death by traveling to the Underworld (175–91). The Chorus conclude the ode by expressing the desire to live a safe life in obscurity (192–201), then turn to announce the arrival of Hercules' human father Amphitryon, Hercules' wife Megara, and their children (202–4).

Some of the Senecan tragedies clearly indicate the identity of the Chorus group; for example, queen Hecuba in *Trojan Women* addresses the Chorus of female Trojan captives as "my people, all you slave-women" (63). The dialogue of the *Hercules Furens* does not make the precise identities of these Chorus members clear, but we assume that they are citizens of Thebes. They also include references to practices such as patronage and lawsuits in the forum (164–6, 172–4) that would be familiar to a Roman audience but would be anachronistic for mythological Thebans. Such anachronisms are common in many genres of Roman mythological poetry. They establish connections between the distant world of the characters and that of the contemporary audience. The Chorus of this play, though not of all the Senecan tragedies, passively observe the action. Its reference to contemporary practices suggests that, like the audience, it is looking at the action from a comparable distance.

Though we should not imagine that the Chorus members have been able to hear Juno's speech, their opening lines provide a counterpoint to the angry goddess's soliloquy in their repeated references to the constellation Ursa Major, the Great Bear (131). Juno also begins her condemnation of Jupiter's mistresses who have been transformed into stars with mention of Ursa Major (6). The Great Bear was once the nymph Callisto, whom Jupiter raped; Juno then transformed her husband's victim into a bear. Many years later, Arcas, Callisto's son by Jupiter, inadvertently shot his mother while out hunting because he did not recognize her in her bear form. Jupiter then transformed both figures into the constellations Ursa Major and Minor, the Great and

Little Bear. The Roman audience would have immediately recognized the myth from Seneca's brief reference, as it was well known from Ovid's influential retelling.[2] As in many of Ovid's stories, Juno appears utterly vicious. She makes the innocent Callisto suffer further after being raped, and tricks Arcas into killing his mother. Though the Chorus cannot yet know it, Juno causes comparable suffering for Hercules and his innocent family on the day of this tragedy. The Chorus's description of the dawn concludes with another unwitting reference to Hercules' fate as the sun rises over Mount Oeta (133). Hercules eventually dies on this mountain, as described in Ovid's *Metamorphoses* (9.152–272) and the pseudo-Senecan tragedy *Hercules on Oeta*.

The lengthy middle section of the ode presents a contrast of city and country life, which was a traditional theme in Roman poetry. Seneca's wealthy audience divided its time between the unhealthy, crowded city of Rome and their opulent country villas. The Roman poets traditionally praised country life for its peace, simplicity, and moral superiority to the corrupt life of the city.[3] The laborers in this ode, the farmer, sailor, and fisherman, aspire to little beyond bare subsistence, and as such live "in innocence—in peace and quiet" (159–60). City-dwellers, however, are engaged in ceaseless competition. The Chorus severely condemn these pursuits: in their view, the mob's favor is "empty," while the lawyer acts "wickedly" in participating in "crazy" cases (171–4). Hercules is engaged in different pursuits, but he has similarly chosen a life in which ambition has taken precedence over peace. His journey to the Underworld, in the Chorus' view, is a particularly significant mistake. He will be there soon enough in the world of the dead, since no human being can avoid it.

The concluding lines of the ode contrast the Chorus members themselves, who seek only tranquil obscurity, with figures who travel the world in pursuit of glory and fame. They do not need to name Hercules as he is the obvious focus of the contrast. They refer to this figure "who rides high up on his chariot" (196), an image that combines both Hercules' passage to Olympus after death and the Roman general who rode through Rome on a chariot in celebration of triumph over defeated enemies.[4] In the Roman triumph, a slave stood beside the victorious general (*triumphator*) and reminded him that he was not a god but a mere mortal. The implication is that Hercules would benefit from the admonitions of such a figure. The final line of the ode is essential to the themes of the play: "Impetuous courage falls from a great height" (201). As is common in tragedy, the Chorus' words have more significance than they can actually know. The remainder of the day that has just dawned will show twice how impetuous courage collapses, first in the case of Lycus and then of Hercules.

Act 2, lines 205–523

Where Hercules' stepmother Juno opened the play by expressing her rage, Hercules' stepfather Amphitryon opens the second act with a lengthy statement of his anxieties regarding his foster son (205–78). The old man laments that Juno has persecuted his son Hercules since infancy, when she attempted to kill him with snakes that the baby crushed in his cradle (205–22). He then lists several of Hercules' Labors (222–48), but laments the fact that his son's success has not brought peace either to the world or to his home, the city of Thebes (249–74). The usurper Lycus has killed Creon, the rightful king, and taken his throne. Amphitryon prays for his son's return to liberate his kingdom (275–8). Hercules' wife Megara extends her father-in-law's brief prayer (279–308). She also prays for Hercules to return from the Underworld in the same way that he overcame other obstacles (279–95), and promises sacrifices to Jupiter and Ceres upon his safe homecoming (295–308). The prayer emphasizes the contrast between Megara's loyalty to her husband, though he has been as abundantly unfaithful to her as Jupiter has been to Juno, and Juno's hostility to Jupiter and Jupiter's illegitimate children. Megara's prayer ends on a note of foreboding, however: she tells Hercules that "you will drag us down" (308) to the Underworld with him. Amphitryon tries to console his daughter-in-law, urging her to remain hopeful. Megara counters, however, that no one can hope to survive so many challenges as Hercules has (309–31).

The arrival of the usurper Lycus interrupts the dialogue between Hercules' father and wife. Lycus introduces himself in a lengthy aside (332–57), not meant to be heard by Amphitryon and Megara.[5] He was previously an ordinary man without distinguished ancestry who usurped the throne of Thebes, and now would gain authority over the people by marrying the noble Megara, daughter of Creon, the former king whom he killed. His interaction with the other characters begins as a grimly amusing effort to court Megara (358–437). Lycus attempts to win over his enemy by suggesting that they should marry in order to bring peace to the troubled city. In outrage, Megara protests that he has killed her father and brothers, taken her family's throne, and will certainly bring upon himself the destruction that typically awaits Theban tyrants such as Oedipus (358–96). Marriage to him is accordingly the last thing on her mind. Lycus shifts from courteous persuasion to an undisguised threat to force Megara to marry him. She retorts that death will be a welcome chance to be reunited with her husband (397–437).

Lycus then turns to argue with Amphitryon that Hercules is not the son of a god but of a human father (438–64). Thus he is no hero, it is appropriate for him to serve Eurystheus as a slave, and he cannot aspire to enter Olympus. Amphitryon apparently feels no shame in Hercules' illegitimacy and takes responsibility for a child whom his wife bore to a god. He retorts that Hercules' Labors prove his divine ancestry and that gods such as Apollo also served temporarily as slaves. Other gods such as Jupiter and Bacchus also had challenging childhoods. The infant Jupiter had to be hidden away from his father Saturn, while Juno destroyed Bacchus' mother Semele before the god could be born and Jupiter had to carry his son to term by sewing him up in his thigh.

Lycus then questions other elements of Hercules' reputation which appear to tell against his heroism, such as his episode in drag at Omphale's court and his kidnapping of the princess Iole, neither the result of Eurystheus' orders to complete the Labors. Amphitryon counters with other examples of Hercules' slaying of monsters on his own initiative (465–89). In frustration, Lycus abandons the argument and commands Megara to marry him. When she refuses, he orders his slaves to burn down the temple where Hercules' family has taken refuge. As Lycus departs to perform a sacrifice to Neptune, Amphitryon calls out to Hercules, and claims to hear his son's arriving footsteps (489–523). Heil convincingly argues that Amphitryon is the victim of his own despairing illusion.[6] No one else, especially not the soldiers who continue to demolish the temple and build the pyre, shares his perceptions. The Act accordingly ends with a vivid tableau that visually emphasizes the family's helplessness and desperate need for rescue by Hercules.

Second Chorus, lines 524–91

The Chorus reprise a theme introduced in the preceding scene by Amphitryon, that Hercules' successful completion of the Labors did not result in a peaceful life. While Eurystheus rules his people without anxieties, Hercules is forced to travel the earth, as far away as distant Scythia (524–46). Now the hero has gone to an even more distant place, the Underworld, and the Chorus urge him to return after conquering death's kingdom as Amphitryon and Megara did in the preceding scene (547–68). The ode ends with an extended comparison between Hercules and Orpheus. The mythical musician successfully interceded with Dis, the god of the Underworld, to be allowed to take his dead wife Eurydice with him back to the world of the living (569–91). In their concluding exhortation, the Chorus claim that Hercules' strength will also conquer death's kingdom like Orpheus's song. But the Chorus also recall that Orpheus lost his wife through his impatience. He did not fulfill Dis's condition that he not look back on his way to the surface to see if his wife was following. Orpheus' true similarity to Hercules will prove to be that both men destroy their loved ones through a fatal lapse at a moment of triumph.

In the Latin script, Seneca uses a different meter in this ode than in the first choral ode. The poet employs the choruses as opportunities to demonstrate his skill and range in a variety of meters. The continuous minor Asclepiads of this ode are "the most vehement" of Seneca's meters, "used to express the sublime, strong contrasts and universal assertions."[7] The metrical choices both build on Horace's experiments with Latin poetic meter and express a connection to the Augustan poet's themes.[8] The Asclepiad meter frequently appears in Horace's lyric collection entitled *Odes*, poems associated like this Chorus with distanced reflection on human failings and the challenges presented by ordinary life. An ode written in continuous Asclepiad lines recalls the opening poem of Horace's *Odes*, which concludes as the Chorus does with a tribute to the power of song. Horace hopes to rise to the stars if his patron Maecenas favors his poetry. The meter recurs in *Odes* 3.30, the poem that concludes Horace's first collection of *Odes*. This poem celebrates Horace's creation of a monument "more lasting than bronze," his collection of poetry that will endure forever and so allow part of him to escape death. When Seneca's Chorus recalls Orpheus' conquest of death through song in an ode that precedes Hercules' return in triumph from the Underworld, both subject and meter evoke Horace's odes on poetic immortality that programmatically enclose his collection of lyric poetry.

Act 3, lines 592–829

The title character has been an absent presence for most of *Hercules Furens*. Others have talked about him at great length, but the audience has not seen him until now. Hercules strides on to the stage with his companion Theseus. He tells the gods of the upper world (except for his enemy Juno) to look away from Cerberus, the three-headed monster that he has just retrieved from the Underworld. Even as Hercules celebrates his triumph in completing Juno's impossible mission, Amphitryon is at first slow to believe his son can have returned alive. His son could be a god, as he hoped at the end of Act 2, or more likely a ghost (592–625). He then quickly relates how Lycus has killed Megara's family and seized the throne. Hercules immediately charges off to kill Lycus, which Theseus claims he has done as fast as he can talk about it (626–45).

Theseus' lengthy narration of his mission to the Underworld comprises the majority of the Act (646–827). After a brief prayer, Theseus describes the Underworld for nearly one hundred lines (prompted by occasional leading questions from Amphitryon), before finally relating what he and Hercules did there (658–759). The arrangement of his speech follows a pattern familiar in ancient rhetorical teaching for describing a scene or individual, a technique that the ancients called *ecphrasis*. His speech describes in leisurely detail: the entrance to the Underworld in Sparta; the rivers Lethe (Forgetfulness) and Cocytus (Mourning); the personifications of evils including Hunger, Fear, and War; the forlorn vegetation and climate of the terrible place; the palace of Dis, god of the Underworld; the judgment of the dead; and the punishment of criminals who offended the gods. Even after Amphitryon eventually asks about Hercules' deed, *ecphrasis* still predominates in Theseus' speech. He describes Charon, the ferryman of the dead, and Cerberus, the three-headed monster (760–91). Only in the final lines of the speech does he relate Hercules' battle with Cerberus and the journey with the monster to the upper world (791–827). Theseus then announces the return of the Chorus to the stage (827–9).[9]

There have been several brief descriptions of Hercules' exotic destinations, such as Iberia and Scythia, so far in the play. Theseus' speech is the lengthiest description of the most exotic of all destinations (see Chapter 2, p. 35ff.). The sheer length of the nearly 100-line description emphasizes the extraordinary achievement of Hercules and Theseus. They are some of the few human beings who have traveled to the Underworld and lived to tell the tale. They have encountered the personifications of Hunger, Fear, Disease, and other ills, but have not been overcome. Another stimulus for the bravura speech comes from literary tradition. The poetry of the preceding generation had made lengthy descriptions of the Underworld a familiar topic, and Seneca takes up the challenge of outdoing his literary ancestors. Virgil's Aeneas, the founder of Rome, travels to the Underworld in the *Aeneid*, as does Ovid's mythical musician Orpheus in the *Metamorphoses*. Both of these underworld travelers in earlier poetry explicitly eschew violence against the residents of the Underworld, but Seneca's Hercules comes there to conquer.

Third Chorus, lines 830–94

The Chorus complement Theseus' lengthy *ecphrasis* of the Underworld in the preceding scene by describing the number and diversity of the dead souls who accompanied the heroes on their journey (830–57). They then speculate on how the dead feel in such a depressing environment, and relate the truisms that death is inevitable and always comes too soon (858–74). The indication that the dead still think, perceive, and feel after death is common in ancient mythological narratives; it is also relevant to the play's philosophical perspectives on suicide (see Chapter 4, p. 89ff.). The meter of the ode up to this point

once more differs from the preceding two. Mazzoli characterizes the
Sapphic line used in this part of the Chorus as "somewhere between
subjective lyricism and philosophical reflection, befit[ting] volatile
and anguished but not yet catastrophic situations."[10] For the second
half of the ode, meter and emotion both change to a shorter glyconic
meter "appropriate for rejoicing and festive occasions."[11] The Chorus
announce the celebrations at Thebes upon Hercules' return now that
he has brought peace to the entire world, including the Underworld
(875–92). As Hercules returns to the stage, they tell him to put a wreath
in his hair and sacrifice in thanksgiving to the gods (892–4).

Act 4, lines 895–1053

Hercules invokes the gods who support him and prepares a sacrifice
to celebrate his killing of Lycus (895–918). His father Amphitryon
reminds him to cleanse his hands, which are still dripping with the
tyrant's blood, and then to ask his divine father Jupiter for peace (918–
52). Hercules prays for the whole earth to be at peace: "may deep
peace feed the people" (929). The hero's prayer implies an extension of
his traditional role as the bringer of peace to individual communities
by slaying the monsters that threaten them. Praying for "deep peace"
for the entire world suggests that all his prior efforts at ridding the
world of evils have been contributions toward this goal. The prayer
also responds to the Chorus' preference for retirement from the world
in the first ode. If Hercules can indeed bring "deep peace" to the world,
then others may be able to choose retirement as well.

At this moment of benevolence, however, Hercules' perception of
the world as others see it falters. He sees an eclipse and believes that
the gods are calling him to overthrow his father Jupiter and rule in
heaven. His hallucinations continue even as his father Amphitryon
attempts to restrain him: Hercules says he sees the Giants storming

Olympus and the Fury attacking him (952–86). At this point, Hercules' misperceptions become lethal. He believes his own children are Lycus's children, and proceeds to shoot at them with his bow. He then storms into the palace, and Amphitryon narrates Hercules' murder of Megara and the children. Hercules then exits the palace, claiming to have offered the victims as sacrifices to Juno, and collapses in a stupor (987–1053). The penultimate act makes good on Juno's threat at the beginning of the play to turn Hercules' powers against himself.

Fourth Chorus, lines 1053–1137

The Chorus react to the violence they have just witnessed by calling on heaven and earth to mourn. They ask the gods to bring peace to Hercules' spirit and let him sleep so his mind may recover from its madness (1053–99). In their view, it will be better for Hercules either to sleep or to stay insane rather than return to a conscious state and recognize what he has done. When he wakes, he will beat himself to signify his remorse, using his strength this time in a literal way against himself (1100–21). Self-directed violence was a traditional part of Greek and Roman mourning ritual. Only at the end of the ode do the Chorus turn to consider some of the victims, the children whose lives have been cut short (1122–37). Not once do they mention Hercules' wife Megara. Their apparent indifference to her death reflects the macho, misogynistic culture in which they and the contemporary Roman audience lived. Hercules will soon remarry and is abundantly unfaithful to each of his wives; his posterity is more important than his partner. This ode returns to the anapaestic meter of the first choral ode, but this use of the meter suggests "contexts where heroic values are overturned and the course of insurmountable events proceeds until the tension comes to a climax."[12] The Chorus likely leave the stage at the end of the final ode and do not return.

Act 5, lines 1138–1344

Hercules wakes but has not yet returned fully to his conscious mind. At first, he does not know where he is, why he sees corpses around him, and why he does not have his weapons (1138–59). When he recognizes that the corpses are those of his wife and children, he does not know who has killed them, or why Theseus and Amphitryon are avoiding his gaze, and he demands to know who has defeated him (1159–86). When Amphitryon does not answer directly, Hercules stretches out his hands to his father and recognizes when he sees the blood upon them that he is the killer (1186–1201). The power of this self-recognition scene depends on the gradual progress of Hercules' emergence from madness. His progressively despairing questions mark his movement from maddened self-alienation to full consciousness of his own deeds and so motivate the lament that follows (1202–29). The Chorus in the preceding ode called on heaven and earth to mourn; Hercules complements their prayer by calling on heaven and earth to destroy him, and seeking to return to the Underworld that he has just left.

Supernumerary characters removed Hercules' weapons at the end of Act 4 as he slept. He now asks for them back in order to kill himself, an act which he characterizes as greater than any of his Labors. The other characters initially refuse to return the weapons: Amphitryon claims it will kill him to see his son die, and Theseus urges him to show courage not by using further violence but by choosing to live on (1229–94). The scene dramatizes a traditional problem in ancient ethics. In his influential essay *On Duties,* composed roughly a century before Seneca's drama, Cicero used the example of returning weapons to an insane person in order to discuss the limitations involved in keeping promises. Cicero observes that "promises are, therefore, sometimes not to be kept; and trusts are not always to be restored. Suppose that a person leaves his sword with you when he is in his right mind, and demands it back in a fit of insanity; it would be criminal to restore it to him; it would be your duty not to do so" (*On Duties* 3.95, tr. Miller).

Seneca includes several examples of this type of "passion-restraint" scene in his tragedies, in which one character announces his or her plan to commit a terrible deed and a less powerful character endeavors to block him or her.[13] The scene derives much of its dramatic tension from the mismatch of the opponents. No one can really stop the world's strongest man from seizing his weapons and doing whatever he wants with them. The challenge that the scene poses is whether Hercules will listen to the father and friend whom he claims to love and respect, or succumb to guilt instead. Wyles has recently emphasized the connection between the restoration of Hercules' weapons and his identity, which has been temporarily altered by his madness: "Above all, Seneca makes use of the idea that Heracles' iconic pieces of costume embody his identity, in order to create the sense of crisis and tension in the final act." Amphitryon's order to remove Hercules' weapons "is intended for his protection, but, in fact, its dramatic effect ... is to strip Heracles of his identity."[14]

In the final movement of the scene (1295–1344), Amphitryon returns Hercules' weapons as he threatens to pull down the palace in order to destroy himself.[15] Hercules draws his bow and trains it on himself; his father tells him that he will die as well if his son does. Hercules yields only when his father puts his sword to his own chest to back up his words. As he wonders where he can go into exile to expiate his crime, Theseus invites him to his kingdom of Athens, a traditional location in myth for harboring guilty fugitives such as Oedipus and Orestes. The play's concluding tableau emphasizes Hercules' reintegration into the community, as his most important moral arbiters, his father and his best friend, stand beside him and certify their forgiveness of him.

2

Major Themes in *Hercules Furens*

Like all of Seneca's tragedies, *Hercules Furens* retells a well-known moment from a famous myth. The ancient audience knew how the tragedy would end before they began watching, as it was an important part of the hero's traditional story. Juno also predicts some of the events that happen during the course of the drama in her opening monologue. What dramatic tension there is in the play does not come from ignorance of the outcome of the events presented on the stage, but from watching the characters work through their conflicts. These conflicts occur primarily in the second and fifth Acts. How will Megara resist Lycus's pressure before Hercules returns? How will Hercules be talked down from suicide?

As the play's lengthy monologues suggest, however, it is rhetoric rather than dramatic tension that forms the major interest of Senecan tragedy.[1] Seneca was the son of a famous rhetorician, and wrote for audiences of aristocrats whose basic education consisted of rhetorical training.[2] All of the themes investigated in this chapter relate to this central interest in rhetoric. Senecan tragedy has justly been called "a drama of the word," one whose richness and exuberance demand public performance of those words.[3] Readers who are fluent in Latin often find themselves reading Seneca's words aloud. Through their lengthy, impassioned speeches, the characters examine what their extreme circumstances reveal about their identities.

Madness and the passions

Modern audiences often evaluate ancient drama using the same sorts of criteria that they apply to contemporary realistic drama: plausibility and consistency of character, motivation, and decision-making. Such criticism is often anachronistic, as it can sometimes involve reading works written two thousand years ago as if they were part of a tradition that did not fully develop in the European theater until the nineteenth century. Yet considerations such as these drive much of the popular agenda surrounding Greco-Roman drama, and inevitably affects the scholarly agenda as well. Audiences respond well to ancient drama in part because they choose to see the characters as similar to themselves rather than members of a foreign and distant culture. Directors have traditionally chosen to accommodate such perspectives, and viewed the very act of staging an ancient drama in the modern world as implicitly conveying the message that the dramatist's power can bridge the gap of time, language, and culture. Hercules' madness accordingly poses a problem for both scholars and popular audiences. Juno talks about turning Hercules against himself, and Hercules claims to see the Fury attacking him, but only once he is already hallucinating (982–6). Seneca does not show a divinity actually attacking his hero on stage, nor does Juno reappear to celebrate her triumph over her enemy like the playwright's other revengers, Atreus and Medea. These choices allow for the possibility that his madness emerges from his violent and ambitious lifestyle. This question of external or internal motivation has been a principal line of division in modern criticism of the play.

One way of approaching the difficulty, though not of resolving it, is to examine Euripides' *Mad Heracles* (*Herakles Mainomenos*), a Greek tragedy of the fifth century BCE which similarly presents the narrative of the hero's return from the Underworld and murder of his family.[4] Euripides' *Heracles* features Lussa, the divine personification of madness, who appears onstage to explain her actions in detail as she drives Heracles mad (*Heracles* 815–74). As this scene has no parallel in Seneca's version, one conclusion that has been drawn from synoptic readings of the plays is that Seneca means to represent internal motivation instead. Scholars such as Fitch who argue for internal motivation note that Hercules' career to date has depended on violence and ambition. As such, the hero comes to regard violence as central to his identity and the first response to any situation.[5] Seneca's Hercules expresses what the ancients called "greatness of spirit" (*magnitudo animi*), which certainly does not endear him to modern audiences who prefer their heroes to serve others modestly. Immediately before he goes mad, for example, he commands heaven and earth as if he were the king of the gods instead of Jupiter (926–39). Other scholars have focused on Hercules' interest in revenge and attempted to minimize the difference that Juno's intervention makes to his character. As Harrison has observed, "his own words and the words others use to describe his actions are very much the same, whether he is sane or insane. He must constantly avenge slights, real or perceived, and administer punishment."[6] These influential readings also conform to the perspective found in contemporary adaptations of both Hercules plays, where the hero has often been viewed as a victim of combat trauma and internal motivation is the dominant explanation for his behavior (see Chapter 5).

As an alternative to the view represented by Fitch and Harrison, others have proposed attention to the figure of Juno and the literary tradition that her appearance at the beginning of the play evokes. Lawall called attention to this tradition as an alternative to "the 'naturalistic' interpretation of Hercules' madness [which] may appeal to twentieth-century psychological critics."[7] By opening the play with an angry Juno, Seneca sends an unmistakable message to his Roman audience that dire persecution of an innocent person will follow. Chapter 4 further examines the angry Juno tradition.

Modern audiences may find Juno's role as a gloating villain unacceptably melodramatic, more reminiscent of the Wicked Witch than of the Roman goddess of marriage. Her speech also appears unacceptably long and bombastic to audiences used to plain speaking and soundbite dialogue. Those who want to understand *Hercules Furens* in its Roman tradition, however, cannot ignore the first tenth of its script.

This is not to simplify the external reading in order to suggest that Juno has made Hercules do something utterly uncharacteristic. Implanting madness in a character in the Roman poetic tradition is more similar to adding a catalyst to a reaction than to flipping an on-off switch. What Juno typically does in Roman epic is accentuate tendencies that already exist in the characters. In Virgil's *Aeneid*, one of Seneca's primary models, the characters already have legitimate reasons to be angry, and the Fury sent by Juno translates those reasons into actions. The Italian champion Turnus does not like losing his promised princess Lavinia to foreigners who have suddenly arrived on his shores, nor does the princess' mother Amata accept her husband's apparently arbitrary decision to engage their daughter to a stranger rather than a family friend (Virgil *Aeneid* 7.286–571). But neither character acts violently upon their frustrations until the Fury's intervention. As the characters of Seneca's tragedy constantly remind the audience, Hercules lives a life of violence. What Juno's assault does is not to transform a peaceful man unexpectedly into a violent one, but to remove a violent man's ability to discriminate between appropriate and inappropriate objects of his violence.

Though Seneca offers a different view of human psychology in his philosophical works, his goals in the play's opening scene reflect his commitment to terms set by prior Roman poetic tradition. Adopting the external perspective on Hercules' madness shifts attention from his decision making, which has been obviated by Juno's divine compulsion, to his reaction after the fact. No matter what his mental state when he committed the murders, he views himself as fully responsible for killing his family. The naturalistic aspect of the drama is accordingly not in the way that the playwright represents descent into madness. Instead, it can be seen in the hero's desire to expiate his guilt by proposing suicide and exile, followed by his reintegration into a community of family and friends.[8]

What then of Hercules' ambitions, implicitly condemned by the Chorus in the first ode? Saying that they are right to seek retirement and Hercules is wrong to be ambitious ignores the dramatic form in which these propositions have been presented. Tragedy characteristically displays characters who present conflicting perspectives, each of which has some merit. The Chorus' praise of retirement is appropriate for ordinary people such as themselves, but not for a hero with divine ancestry who is also the victim of divine persecution. Hercules can concurrently pursue personal glory while endeavoring to benefit the communities that are no longer threatened by the monsters that he has destroyed. While his commands to heaven and earth (926–39) may indeed represent an example of arrogant "overreaching," it is still worth noticing that his vision of a prosperous world without war or tyranny is far more desirable than the troubled place actually ruled by his father Jupiter. Juno's fear of Hercules' ambition reflects her position as a vengeful wife, and Lycus's derision of the hero's accomplishments is part of his (incorrect) calculation that he can take over Thebes because there will be none to oppose him. Hercules' family, Amphitryon and Megara, express their love for him by praising his ambitious fulfillment of the Labors, even if his absence has brought them mortal danger. As Billerbeck justly observes, "it is entirely consistent if Juno interprets as megalomania and arrogance those qualities that Megara and Amphitryon praise as virtues."[9] The dramatic point of the controversy over Hercules' career is to set each character's views in conflict with another's. It is accordingly inappropriate to reject any of these four perspectives completely.

Hercules' episode of madness does have some relationship to his prior lifestyle, but not in the sense that his prior acts of violence inevitably compel him to murder his family. While mad, Hercules sees a world visible only to himself. He believes that an eclipse reveals the victims of his Labors in the sky (the Nemean lion, the Cretan bull) and the gods welcoming him into Olympus, until they turn to war with the Giants (939–86). His hallucinations develop Juno's earlier, personalized view of the sky to an extreme. Where she saw a sky full of her particular obsessions, her husband's rape victims, Hercules sees one that reflects his triumphs and ambitions (the Labors, rule in Olympus). Where the Fury supplies the triggering event that pushes Hercules into violence against his family, the hero's prior career supplies the content of his hallucinations. Hercules' destructive rage shows anger's relation to misperception as well as its most extreme consequences. What the ancients called the "passions" differ considerably from our modern folk narratives of character formation. In their view, anger was the worst of the passions, and a form of temporary madness (see Chapter 4, p. 84ff.).[10] Both in *Hercules Furens* and in other plays, Seneca uses the connection between violence and madness to explore extreme aspects of character.

Courage, violence, and suicide

The final line of the first choral ode is one of the most important in the play: "Impetuous courage falls from a great height" (201). The play dramatizes this fall twice over: Lycus boldly seizes the throne, and is killed by Hercules; Hercules returns from the greatest of his Labors, only to render them valueless by killing his family. The word that Wilson translates as "courage" is *virtus*, from which English derives the word "virtue." Contemporary English speakers understand this word to mean "a moral quality regarded as good or desirable in a person,

such as patience, kindness, etc.; a particular form of moral excellence."[11]
But the root of the Latin word is *vir,* meaning "man," cognate with
English words such as "virile." *Virtus* accordingly denotes in Latin
"manly spirit, resolution, valour, steadfastness ... esp. as displayed in
war and other contests."[12] At one point (340), Wilson translates *virtus*
equally accurately as "machismo." Hercules' *virtus* is his strength and
courage, and he does not have to exemplify our culture's other-directed
virtues (patience, kindness, moral excellence, etc.) to possess what the
Romans would have called *virtus.*

As in many works of ancient literature concerned with the deeds of
heroes, a major concern of *Hercules Furens* is the definition of *virtus*
and its appropriate applications. The debate over its meaning begins in
Act 2, when Amphitryon observes that some people "give the name of
virtue / to successful crime" (251–2), in this case Lycus's illegal seizure
of power. Lycus no less than Hercules perceives his *virtus* as intrinsic
to his identity. Both are courageous risk-takers, though they turn these
aspects of their personalities toward different goals. The tyrant sees
himself as "famous for machismo" (340), and thus ambitious enough
to seize the throne in the absence of a legitimate claim or noble
ancestry. The Chorus' words about the collapse of *virtus* apply with
even greater justice to him. Strength and courage are best illustrated
through challenge, as in Megara's question, "If there were no hard
commands, what place for courage?" (433) when Lycus attempts to
disdain Hercules as a slave who must carry out others' commands.
Strength and courage have appropriate limitations, however. Aristotle
defined them, like the other virtues, as a mean between two extremes.[13]
To murder one's family while mad may take some physical strength
but is in no sense an expression of *virtus.* The Chorus make this
distinction clear in the final ode: after Hercules has collapsed in a
stupor, they pray "let *virtus* and dutifulness return to the man" (1093,
my translation). When Hercules desires to commit suicide once he
recognizes his guilt, Theseus exhorts him to turn his *virtus* to a new

purpose, that of self-control: "now is the time / to use your heroic courage; Hercules must not stay angry" (1276–77). Hercules eventually agrees that the *virtus* that pushes him to suicide must yield to his dutifulness. He must obey his father's order to live on, or risk killing his father as well (1315). Heroism based on strength and courage may have granted Hercules one form of success, but it has significant limitations. If he is unable to master himself, there are important senses in which his ability to master others does not matter. In his philosophical writings, Seneca subjects traditional notions of power, strength, and courage to a similar critique (see Chapter 4, p. 87ff.).

The Chorus criticize Hercules for his ambitious pursuit of *virtus* in the first ode, in contrast to their own preference for retirement from the world. Many readers have taken their verdict as definitive and "objective."[14] On this view, Hercules' madness is the inevitable outcome of a violent, ambitious lifestyle, and the play comes to resemble a narrative of arrogance punished. Earlier scholars attempted to relate the praise of the simple country life, a motif common in several Senecan choruses, to the period of his career that he spent in exile on Corsica. Such naive biographical interpretation used to be common in criticism of Roman poetry but does not offer much help in reading a literary artist who was a master of multiple voices and perspectives. The praise of the virtuous countryside is also not particular to Seneca but a basic motif in Roman poetry. The motif was so well known that the Augustan poet Horace could parody it in his second *Epode,* and Ovid could represent the countryside in the *Metamorphoses* as the favored location for rapes by the gods. Attention to the literary tradition behind this ode suggests that the Chorus' words are not authoritative but simply one of many perspectives on offer in the tragedy.

More recent readers have accordingly observed (more accurately, in my view) that this traditionally dominant interpretation of the play ignores the role of Juno. If the point is to show a man punished for his arrogance and ambition, then it is hard to see the purpose of the play's monumental opening speech by Juno.[15] The "deserved punishment" reading also ignores the effects of Juno's endless persecution of Hercules, which Amphitryon emphasizes immediately following the first choral ode (205–22). Hercules was born to run: he slew his first monster in his cradle when Juno sent serpents to kill him, and he completed the Labors under Eurystheus' orders. Thus he can hardly be said to have made a free choice to undertake his heroic career. The Chorus also pity Hercules for his madness after he kills the children (1053–1121), rather than condemning him as a man who would murder his loved ones due to a characteristic lack of self-control.

Seneca's examination of the ambiguities of *virtus* reflects the interests of his times. One need look no further than his nephew Lucan, who criticized the epic tradition's typical praise of *virtus* in his *Civil War*, an epic narrating the first eighteen months of the war between Caesar and Pompey from its outbreak in 49 BCE. The poem's opening lines condemn the Romans of the previous century who "turned their victorious right hands against their own vitals . . . kindred fought against kindred" (*Civil War* 1.3–4, tr. Duff). Like Hercules killing his family and then proposing to kill himself, the Romans used their force against themselves and their own family members when they engaged in civil war. Victory celebrations in civil war are tainted by the fact that one's own people are the enemy, and so *virtus* has been evacuated of its symbolic meaning.[16]

Lucan investigates a different model of heroism, that of endurance and opposition to tyranny, in the figure of the loyalist general Cato. After Pompey's defeat in 48 BCE, the historical Cato unsuccessfully opposed Caesar by taking his men on a taxing march through the deserts of North Africa that culminated in his suicide at Utica. This famous refusal to surrender to a tyrant made "Cato of Utica" an attractive figure for allegorists, including Seneca (see Chapter 4, p. 79ff.). Elements of Cato's march across North Africa recalled Hercules' journey to recover the Hesperides' apples.[17] In Lucan, however, Cato appears as a parodic figure of ascetic excess. His remarriage to his wife Marcia is a sterile reversal of the Roman wedding ceremony, and he subjects both himself and his men to hyperbolic extremes of self-denial on their dangerous march through the desert. Seneca's Hercules is a more congenial model of endurance in the face of adversity.

After he realizes that he has killed his family, Hercules proposes to commit suicide in order to escape his guilt. As Amphitryon and Theseus try to calm him, he cries out, "bring me my arms, let my hands / take revenge on Fortune" (1271–2). On numerous occasions in his philosophical writings, Seneca recommends committing suicide when misfortune has left people in a situation when they can no longer live freely. He gives the example of a captured German sent to fight wild beasts in the arena games, who took control of the manner of his death by choking himself with a toilet brush:

> There was lately in a training-school for wild-beast gladiators a German, who was making ready for the morning exhibition; he withdrew in order to relieve himself—the only thing which he was allowed to do in secret and without the presence of a guard. While so engaged, he seized the stick of wood, tipped with a sponge, which was devoted to the vilest uses, and stuffed it, just as it was, down his throat; thus he blocked up his windpipe, and choked the breath from his body. That was truly to insult death! Yes, indeed; it was not a very elegant or becoming way to die; but what is more foolish than to be over-nice about dying? What a brave fellow! He surely deserved to be allowed to choose his fate! How bravely he would have wielded a sword! With what courage he would have hurled himself into the depths of the sea, or down a precipice! Cut off from resources on every hand, he yet found a way to furnish himself with death, and with a weapon for death. Hence you can understand that nothing but the will need postpone death. Let each man judge the deed of this most zealous fellow as he likes, provided we agree on this point,—that the foulest death is preferable to the fairest slavery.
>
> Seneca, *Moral Letters* 70.20–1, tr. Gummere

Seneca praises the German captive, a man on the opposite end of the social scale from himself, for his act of courage aimed at securing autonomy. Even though the German captive has no control over his life, he can nevertheless escape slavery by choosing how and when to die. This principle is at the core of Stoic thinking on autonomy. This fundamental aspect of self-control can never be taken away from a person, no matter how unfortunate their circumstances have become. As Megara observes to Lycus when he attempts to force her into marriage, "One who can be forced does not know how to die" (426, tr. Fitch). Some Roman aristocrats concurred with the Stoic philosophers on viewing suicide as a means of avoiding dishonor.[18] Like Seneca, some would also be ordered to commit suicide by the emperor. This form of death avoided the disgrace of the alternative, a public execution, and also sometimes permitted their families to inherit their estates.

Hercules Furens Act 5, however, examines suicide from a different perspective when Amphitryon and Theseus succeed in getting Hercules to think about someone other than himself. While Hercules feels great guilt after killing his family, the reasons for which the Stoics typically approved suicide do not pertain. Shame is not an issue, as the community represented by the Chorus and the characters have absolved him. His autonomy is not at issue either, as he has completed the Labors and is no longer a slave to Eurystheus. From the Stoic perspective, his duty to others takes precedence over his desire to escape his emotional pain through suicide.[19] In one of his philosophical letters, Seneca explains how he suffered episodes of ill-health that made him want to end his life. Yet he elected to remain alive because of his love for his father:

> For when I was still young, I could put up with hardships and show a
> bold front to illness. But I finally succumbed, and arrived at such a
> state that I could do nothing but snuffle, reduced as I was to the
> extremity of thinness. I often entertained the impulse of ending my
> life then and there; but the thought of my kind old father kept me

back. For I reflected not how bravely I had the power to die, but how
little power he had to bear bravely the loss of me. And so I commanded
myself to live. For sometimes it is an act of bravery even to live.

Seneca, Moral Letters 78.1–2, tr. Gummere

Attentiveness to others' needs, not autonomy, is the point of connection
between the sickly Seneca and the robust Hercules. For the hero of the
Labors, true *virtus* involves living on at the request of his father and
friend, no matter how courageous his suicide would have appeared. His
divine enemy has brought him misfortune: Fischer observes that Juno
plays the role of "an allegorical figure of fortune because her attitude
towards Hercules correlates with Seneca's philosophical conception of
fortune as a challenge for men."[20] Yet as Seneca and the other Stoics
frequently observe, it would be cowardice to yield to Juno as it would be
to yield to any misfortune.

Ancestry and identity

The family provided a major component of an elite Roman's social
identity, as it did for aristocrats in many traditional societies. Whatever
a Roman aristocrat did (or failed to do) would be judged by his peers
in terms of its augmentation or diminution of the prestige of the
family name. A famous family name could provide a Roman with
powerful assets, and elite Romans accordingly applied energy and
creativity toward presenting their ancestry in the best possible light.
Families would present the deeds of famous ancestors, even legendary
ones, in a variety of media: public speeches, exemplary literature,
funeral processions, statuary, coins, and so on.[21] Yet by Seneca's day, the
same small group of elite families no longer handed down wealth and
power to their children as they had under the Republic. The Julio-
Claudian emperors now controlled Roman politics, and a successful
public career depended upon imperial favor. The emperors often chose

to consolidate their power by elevating men without distinguished ancestry. Such men could be more likely trusted in part because they owed their power to the emperor. A member of the traditional aristocracy, by contrast, might regard the emperor in this early period of the Empire as a competitor for privileges that had traditionally belonged to his own family.

Seneca's own family offers a ready example of this cultural shift. His father moved the family from Spain to Rome when Seneca was a child, and became a famous rhetorician (see Chapter 4, p. 65ff.). The elder Seneca became a member of the order of knights (*equites*), the lower rank of the Roman nobility. Nothing about his career, however, suggested that his son would become, for a time, the second most powerful man in the Roman world. The younger Seneca's rise and fall was due to his skill as a rhetorician, author, and courtier rather than to his father's name. Seneca's varied career is an extreme example of a broader transition among the Roman aristocracy as the result of the monopolization of power by Rome's first imperial dynasty, the Julio-Claudian emperors. Many of his philosophical writings are efforts to reorient the ethical perspective of his class.

In *Hercules Furens,* Seneca guides a contemporary audience of Roman aristocrats to reflect on this changed meaning of family. The first words of the play, spoken by Juno, introduce the connection between family identity and identity as an individual. In mythological tradition, Juno is both sister and wife of Jupiter. For the ancients, the incestuousness of their relationship was a less significant component of the story than the notion of parity. The supreme god can only marry his equal, and only his sibling could be equal to him. But thanks to her husband's endless adulteries, Seneca's Juno complains that she is now "sister of the Thunderer—only his sister" (1), rather than Jupiter's legitimate wife. As the most distinguished of Jupiter's illegitimate children, Hercules poses an unacceptable threat to Juno. If he is able to resist her, he might be able to overthrow his father and take control of

Olympus, whereupon she would be deprived of any power she derives from being Jupiter's wife (63–74). Juno engages in paranoid exaggeration rather than stating objective facts, but also thinks like a traditional Roman aristocrat. She views Hercules' claims to power as deriving primarily from his paternity.

In the act that follows, Amphitryon presents a gentler view of ancestry that contrasts sharply with Juno's rage. Hercules' human father loves a son whom he knows is not his own but Jupiter's. His peaceful acceptance of the situation contrasts with the reactions of other Senecan characters, who respond even to the suspicion of adultery with murderous violence. Theseus in *Phaedra* (945–58) curses his son Hippolytus because he incorrectly suspects him of raping his stepmother Phaedra. Atreus in *Thyestes* (234–43) fears that his sons may have actually been fathered by his brother, and takes revenge by killing his brother's sons and feeding them to him. Amphitryon feels no disgrace at raising an illegitimate child, nor does he feel threatened by Hercules' superior powers. He is instead content that his son has been able to marry into a better family, and praises Megara as "partner of my blood" (309, my translation). Amphitryon's relaxed attitude toward ancestry helps him to forgive Hercules readily for the murder of the children rather than condemn him for destroying his line of descent.

Family terminology is a serious matter for Seneca's characters: they will often avoid proper names and address one another with family terms in order to emphasize particular aspects of the identity conferred by the relationship.[22] Seneca typically uses the pattern of defining identity through family relationship with ironic point. The best-known example is Phaedra's insistence that her stepson Hippolytus should address her as sister or slave rather than mother (*Phaedra* 609–12). Being reminded of her role as the young man's stepmother emphasizes the impossibility of fulfilling her incestuous desire. In *Hercules Furens*, Amphitryon refers to Dis as Hercules' uncle (because he is Jupiter's brother), and asks Theseus if he had given him Cerberus willingly (761). The irony here is that the lord of the Underworld shows no favor to anyone, even close family. Hercules thinks in terms of ancestry in the same way as the other characters. One of his first assumptions when waking from his stupor is that if he has been defeated and stripped of his weapons, it must be because his father Jupiter chose to engender a greater child than him (1157–9). As in most examples of Senecan tragic irony, the character says more than he or she knows. Hercules has indeed been defeated by one of Jupiter's children, but it is himself rather than another.

Many members of Seneca's audience were wealthy and powerful, but it was likely that most of them could not claim noble birth. As Saller observed in a demographic study of the Roman elite of the early empire, "most senators ... could not boast a long, illustrious agnatic [descent through males] lineage, nor was there the same need for a great *nomen* [family name] since its recognition in the assemblies was no longer of political consequence."[23] The Lycus scene dramatizes some of the views of the contemporary Roman elite on the value of ancestry and subjects them to criticism. Lycus introduces himself as a man without distinguished ancestry, but nevertheless as ambitious enough to seize the throne of Thebes in spite of this seemingly obvious bar to legitimate rule. He praises himself for working hard to steal what he now has rather than "lazily inheriting the kingdom / from my father's house" (337–8). Megara appears to confirm Lycus's notion that ancestry is no benefit when she recalls the traditional crimes and punishments of the Theban royals (386–96). Oedipus killed his father and married his mother; his sons fought a civil war over his throne; Cadmus was turned into a snake. Megara hopes that Lycus's story will end with an equally gruesome punishment, even though he is not a descendant of the royal house. On Lycus's view, it might well be better to be an outsider bringing in new blood than to suffer the inherited curse of the Theban dynasty.

Lycus's meritocratic views on the value of work and self-reliance rather than living on inherited wealth might initially appear congenial to a modern audience, no less than to the self-made men in Seneca's audience. Congenial, that is, until we recall that Lycus is a villain, and the "work" that he refers to means killing innocent people and seizing their possessions. Such considerations also apply to Hercules and his Labors. Hercules too is an outsider (his father Amphitryon was born in Tiryns) who has gained rule of Thebes by marrying Megara. Lycus points out near the end of the scene that Hercules has also used his strength to victimize innocents. Without Juno's instigation, he raped the princess Iole and (in some versions of the story) killed her father Eurytus (477–80). The work that Hercules performs to gain glory is similarly killing and stealing, no different in kind from Lycus's. The only difference is that we do not receive a sympathetic view of Hercules' other victims in this play, or indeed in most of the stories about the hero.

Lycus intends to marry Megara not to gain the throne of Thebes, which he already possesses, but to consolidate his power by improving his popularity and thereby minimizing the threat of armed revolution: "Regimes are unstable when the ruler / does not belong . . . [Megara's] famous forebears will paint / my unknown family a better colour" (344–5, 347–8). In his view, ancestry is at base a public relations asset. The gullible citizens who care about such appearances may find him more acceptable if he marries the queen, and ignore the fact that the true basis of his rule is military power. Lycus knows that what really matters is what he does, rather than who his parents were, but most men are too foolish to perceive this. Lycus is a villainous tyrant, but Seneca has worse on offer in other plays. Atreus, the tyrant of *Thyestes*, does not even try to pacify the people with the appearance of virtuous behavior.[24] Like Lycus's self-satisfied praise of his hard "work" of violent usurpation, the statement of values may be accurate in an abstract sense, but it is invalidated by the character of its speaker and the context in which he says it.

Seneca similarly discusses popular misperceptions of the importance of noble ancestry in one of his *Moral Letters*. When his addressee Lucilius complains that he has been born too low and has not achieved enough success in life thanks to his bad luck, Seneca counters that philosophy has the power to elevate him: "If there is any good in philosophy, it is this—that it never looks into pedigrees ... A noble mind is free to all men; according to this test, we may all gain distinction."[25] Furthermore, if Lucilius should elect to become a philosopher, then he may choose as his symbolic ancestors the great philosophers of the past, such as Socrates, Plato, and Cleanthes, and he will achieve true nobility if he behaves in a manner worthy of their tradition.[26] Here the realistic context and the congeniality of the speaker support the argument, rather than undermine it as in the Lycus scene. Very few people, whether in Seneca's day or now, are content in the belief that they have been born lucky or achieved enough in their lives. The offer of the philosophical life provides a welcome consolation. Disaffected elites can acquire distinguished (symbolic) ancestry and accomplish achievements in the personal sphere if they find themselves blocked in the public sphere. Seneca makes the argument to both philosophical and tragic audiences that ancestry can be an asset but not an indispensable one.

Proof of ancestry's dispensability in *Hercules Furens* comes when Lycus abandons his plan to marry Megara once she makes clear she will not have him, and decides to kill her and the rest of her family instead (501–8). In the final part of the scene, Lycus challenges the identification of Hercules as son of Jupiter and argues that the hero is only the son of his human father Amphitryon. The man without noble ancestry has an outsider's critical perspective on those who would claim divine connections. He selects aspects of Hercules' career that indicate to his satisfaction that the hero cannot be the son of a god, such as his persecution by Juno, his enslavement to Eurystheus, his episode of transvestism, and his (apparent) entrapment in the

Underworld (422–71). As discussed above, Amphitryon gladly accepts the role of confessed cuckold rather than discredit Hercules, and argues against each of Lycus's charges. Hercules' triumphant return from the Underworld and immediate killing of Lycus serve as the final disproof of Lycus's criticisms. Hercules' next act is to kill his own family, however, and his hallucinatory ravings appear to confirm some of Juno's fears when he threatens to overthrow Jupiter and rule in Olympus (955–73). Confirming that Lycus is a liar, therefore, does not mean that Hercules' divine ancestry is necessarily a good. It may have enabled him to complete the Labors, but it has not brought him a happy or stable life and it has resulted in death and suffering for his loved ones.

The meaning of ancestry becomes a subject of debate in the play's final scene, when Hercules proposes to commit suicide to escape from his guilt in killing his family. Amphitryon is only able to prevent the hero from carrying through on his plan by threatening to kill himself first (1302–13). This action turns on the argument he has been making throughout the play, that Hercules is the biological son of Jupiter but the emotional son of Amphitryon. Ancestry has been reinterpreted here as a combination of blood and intention. Jupiter's biological paternity enables Hercules to be a hero, but Amphitryon's paternity gives him social identity and life-saving emotional connections. Amphitryon in turn derives glory through his connection to Hercules. Amphitryon's embrace of his step-parenthood reflects one response among the Roman aristocracy to its failure to reproduce its political power consistently. This was a renewed interest in adoption, fosterage, and other kinds of family-like connections. If a noble family could not produce a son, or could not set that son on a successful political career, adoption might help to solve the problem.[27] Through their conflicts, the characters of *Hercules Furens* dramatize many of the questions regarding the value of ancestry that Seneca's audience were working through in their social lives.

Moralized landscapes

This section examines a few of the narrative and ethical purposes to which Seneca puts the lengthy descriptions of place in *Hercules Furens*. How characters see the world around them reflects their moral and emotional states. Juno sees the night sky as a battleground populated by Jupiter's rape victims, and says she has come unwillingly to earth after they have exiled her from heaven (1–18). But Thebes provides no sense of refuge for her, as it is the place where Jupiter has engendered numerous illegitimate offspring, worst of all Hercules (19–22). Juno transforms what should be neutral features of the night sky into personified aggressors. Her report on Hercules' return from the Underworld to Thebes is comparably skewed and self-interested: she claims that "when Cerberus is seen, day slips and Sun is scared" (60). The claims she makes about the landscape show that she does not appear to share the same perceptions of the physical world as the other characters. Though Hercules tells the gods to look away from Cerberus, no other character observes any form of disturbance as a result of the monster's arrival in the upper world. Like her enemy Hercules, who suffers from hallucinations, Juno too has a private view of the world, one that reflects her outsized jealousy and rage. The Chorus's descriptions of the landscape conflict with Juno's from the opening words of the first ode. Immediately following the goddess's tirade, the Chorus describe the dawning day in terms of peace and moral goodness, the opposite of Juno's insistence that the sky has been filled with Jupiter's depravity. The Chorus's odes may be monologues, but that does not mean that they are emotionally or intellectually static. Instead, they provide opportunities for dramatic conflict with the positions taken by the characters.

The Chorus contrast the peaceful countryside where virtue flourishes with the corrupting city where ambitious men pursue misguided goals (see Chapter 1, p. 3ff.). The comparison responds to a similar passage of Euripides' *Phaethon*, a tragedy that survives to us only in

brief excerpts quoted in other authors.[28] Phaethon attempted to drive
the chariot belonging to his father, the Sun god, across the sky. His
failure to control the horses led to his own death and to widespread
destruction when the sun came too close to the world. The conservative,
tradition-bound ancients used the Phaethon story as a moral example
of the dangers of excessive ambition, of usurping one's father's position
too soon, and the likelihood of failure when reaching above one's
predetermined social position. Euripides' young, ambitious Phaethon
receives a warning about taking on a task too great for him, similarly
expressed in terms of the contrast between the virtuous country life
and the corrupting city life. Due to his ambitious courage, he also
literally falls from the height of the sky. Yet Phaethon chose a task too
great for him on his own initiative, while Hercules was forced to
complete the Labors, a fact the Chorus later acknowledge. When the
Chorus warn Hercules about his overreaching, then, they overlook this
crucial ethical difference.

Seneca idealizes, exaggerates, and moralizes his literary landscapes
inhabited by the farmers, sailors, city-dwellers, and ordinary Thebans.
The main goal of these descriptions of landscape (*ecphrases*) is to
recall the relevant mythological backgrounds and ethical associations
for the audience, not to accurately depict a mundane, recognizable
reality.[29] The landscape around Thebes is important only insofar as it
evokes particular kinds of mythological associations that contribute
to the play's overall themes. Thus the sun rises not over any generic
thickets, but those "known for Pentheus' death" (135), and the call of
the nightingale similarly recalls Tereus' rape of Philomela (139–41).
These stories of madness, family violence, and mythological challenge
to the gods, reflect indirectly on Hercules' story. Pentheus, an earlier
king of Thebes, challenged the authority of the god Bacchus, was
driven mad, and was killed by his female relatives. The Athenian
princess Procne avenged her sister Philomela's rape by murdering her
children by the Thracian king Tereus. Seneca distributes comparable

motifs throughout his Hercules narrative. Lycus challenges Hercules' identity as the son of a god and is duly punished, while Hercules is driven mad in punishment for his putative challenge to Juno and kills his family.

The second choral ode adds a third term to the city/country contrast of the first ode by narrating Hercules' journey through remote and dangerous places. The Chorus's descriptions of Scythia and the Underworld (533–57) present them as places where no sane person would go. In their view, Hercules' fate is even more pitiful than those of the ambitious city-dwellers of the first ode, as he did not choose to undertake his journey (524–7). Some ancient geographers located the Scythians in southern Russia, but geographical reality was not the main point for most mythological narratives. Rather, Scythia offers a conceptual contrast to Greco-Roman conventions of thought. The Scythians live in a climate and terrain that are extreme by Mediterranean standards. Seneca's Chorus claim that the sea is frozen most of the year, and other narratives represent the Scythians as nomads who subsist on meat and milk, rather than agriculturalists who plant vines and grain.[30] The fictional Amazons, warrior women who live independently of men, present an even stronger contrast with the ancient Mediterranean norm. References to distance, extreme challenge, and exotic customs all emphasize Hercules' role as a world conqueror, an important part of his role as a model for rulers (see Chapter 3, p. 56ff.).

Hercules not only travels over the furthest reaches of the earth, but also transforms the landscape in the course of his Labors. In Act 2, Amphitryon and Megara describe Hercules' extraordinary feats at Gibraltar in southern Spain and in the vale of Tempe in Greece. Hercules traveled to the Atlantic coast of Iberia in order to kill the three-bodied monster Geryon. While passing south to Libya, he created the Straits of Gibraltar. In Amphitryon's words, "he burst the mountains open. Into the gulf / he made a highway for the rushing ocean" (237–8). The earliest mythological accounts only had Hercules setting up the "Pillars of Hercules" at Gibraltar to represent the western boundary of the world.[31] Later in the scene, Megara describes Hercules' feat of opening the Tempe pass, "cracking open hilltops to find the river's path, / and it gushed forth when all Tempe ... / exploded and lay open ... the rushing river [Peneus] flowed on a new bed" (284–8). Hercules' power over nature is godlike: in the same way that he can carry the entire world on his mighty shoulders (69–70), he affects the natural landscape as no human beings could. These recollections of his earlier feats encourage Amphitryon and Megara to believe that Hercules can break through the barrier of the Underworld and return to them—but also confirm Juno's fears that he may take over heaven.

Scythia represents the strangest and most distant place that an adventurer can go on earth, and so only a place not on this earth could outdo such a journey. The journey to the Underworld sets Hercules not only against death, mankind's greatest challenge, but also against challenges to his moral condition. Theseus' description of the geography of the Underworld and its inhabitants is the play's most fully elaborated descriptive speech (658–827). As Theseus relates, the Underworld harbors personifications of evil that may affect Hercules (689–96). His strength and divine ancestry may protect him against Sleep, Hunger, and Old Age.[32] Yet he is the victim of Shame, Grief, and "gnashing Resentment" as the result of his own actions after his return to the surface.[33] Juno accentuates these threats by promising to summon further personifications from the Underworld to attack Hercules, including "hated Crime," "savage Treachery," "Madness, and Passion, / always armed against itself" (96–9). When Hercules finally brings Cerberus to the surface, he orders the gods to look away from the morally polluting sight of the Underworld monster (592–604). The Underworld is also a place where the wicked are punished. Virgil's Sibyl hurries the dutiful Aeneas away from this part of the Underworld, on the grounds that "no pure person is permitted to tread the criminals' threshhold" (*Aeneid* 6.563). Seneca's Theseus, however, claims that he and Hercules actually saw the punishment of criminals, tyrants, and the impious opponents of the gods (731–59), and accordingly ran the risk of the corruption that Virgil's Sibyl feared. In Seneca's presentation, then, the Underworld is the place where Hercules performs the ultimate display of courage and physical strength, but also leaves himself open to insidious assaults on his moral center. Trinacty has recently emphasized the speech's thematic function: "to stress Hercules' fleeting victory over death and to blur the worlds of the living and the dead, thus foreshadowing the conclusion of the play and Hercules' final death wish."[34] The speech expands on the view propounded more briefly in the first ode that Hercules should not hurry to the Underworld, as all human beings will come there soon enough.

After the murders, Hercules collapses and then wakes at the beginning of Act 5 claiming not to know where he is (1138–42). The opening of the act dramatizes what may be Hercules' slow return to sanity, but more likely represents his inability to immediately confront the truth of what he has done. After admitting his responsibility for the murders, he describes a series of dangerous landscapes in which he could undergo appropriate punishment. He could suffer exposure on the Caucasus like the Titan Prometheus, who was punished for stealing fire from heaven, or he could be crushed between the Clashing Rocks that stood at the entrance to the Black Sea (1206–15). While still contemplating suicide but as yet denied his weapons, Hercules wants to take first the whole region of Thebes, and then the whole world with him (1284–94). When Amphitryon talks his son down from suicide, Hercules seeks next to disappear into exile. This is certainly a lighter penalty, but not one without consequences in the ancient world. Exiles typically suffered prejudice and social marginalization when they moved to new cities. Amphitryon earlier derides Lycus as an exile (269–74), imputing thereby that the tyrant engaged in criminal behavior prior to his current crime of usurpation. Yet Hercules still regards exile as an insufficient penalty. No place can expiate his crime, and he cannot be exiled in any event because he is known throughout the world (1321–31). Hercules' catalog of extreme landscapes expresses a version of his characteristic greatness of spirit: the world is simply not big enough for him.

In the play's concluding lines, Theseus responds to Hercules' despair at finding an appropriate place for exile by offering sanctuary in his kingdom of Athens. This offer reprises the king's traditional role in Athenian tragedy of offering shelter to exiles such as Oedipus and the victims of the Theban civil war. Like the other Athenian playwrights, Euripides offers extensive praise of his home city of Athens in the Theseus scene at the conclusion of his *Heracles.* Seneca omits the praise of Athens in a tragedy written for Romans; yet however briefly he presents the motif, it is emphasized by its concluding position. Athens will serve Hercules as a place where, thanks to Theseus' hospitality and friendship, he may begin to recreate the social bonds that he has destroyed and forget the horror of Thebes. Even though the audience knows Hercules will not ultimately settle there but will continue to wander in search of adventure, it is the best ethical landscape for ordinary people such as themselves.

3

Monster-slayer, Moral Exemplar, and Madman: Hercules' Ancient Roles

Hercules is the best-known figure in classical mythology. The literary and artistic tradition created before Seneca involving the hero was immense. The *Lexicon Iconographicum Mythologiae Classicae*, a standard reference work on ancient mythological art, lists nearly 4,000 images of Hercules.[1] The hero's manifold career as monster-slayer, traveler, captive slave, family man, and lover lent itself to innumerable variations. Seneca's audience would have understood the particular episode related in *Hercules Furens* as one of many possible selections from his heroic career. This chapter surveys some of the previous representations of Hercules available to the Roman audience of Seneca's drama.

Juno's hostility to Hercules and her fear that he will depose his father Jupiter and rule in heaven are features of the hero's story present from the beginning of the Greco-Roman poetic tradition. In Homer's *Iliad*, Diomedes transcends the normal limits of human combat and wounds the goddess Aphrodite on the battlefield. The goddess of love returns in anger to Olympus, where her mother Dione attempts to console her with the thought that other gods have also suffered at human hands. She tells her that Hercules shot both Hera in the breast and Hades in the shoulder with his bow, and concludes: "Heracles was simply outrageous and reckless / to provoke the Olympian gods with arrows" (*Iliad* 5.403–4, tr. Lombardo).[2] Seneca omits any reference to Hercules' ability to revenge himself directly on Juno. His hero instead triumphs through endurance, while Juno's challenges increase his fame.

The journey to the Underworld was traditionally Hercules' greatest Labor, and thus posed a consummate challenge for other mythological heroes. Could they master death in the way that he had? For Theseus, the answer was no; Hercules had to rescue him and his friend Pirithous instead. Nor was Theseus' mission in any sense as glorious as Hercules'. He had come on his own initiative to carry off Persephone, the wife of Dis, god of the Underworld. The mythical musician Orpheus succeeded in persuading Dis to let his dead wife Eurydice live again but failed to bring her to the surface. Homer's *Odyssey* offers a different point of comparison between Hercules and other heroes. Odysseus encounters Heracles' phantom in the Underworld, a stand-in for the hero who had already joined the other gods on Olympus. Heracles offers his sympathy to the wandering hero, claiming that both he and Odysseus have been made to suffer despite their excellence (*Odyssey* 11.617–26). Though Homer's Heracles speaks very briefly, these words inaugurate a new way of looking at the hero, as a man famous for his endurance of sufferings as much as for his triumph over enemies. This theme dominates the final act of Seneca's tragedy, in which both Amphitryon and Theseus teach Hercules to accept his suffering and live on rather than escape in suicide.

Madman and child-killer: Euripides' *Mad Heracles* (*Herakles Mainomenos*)

Euripides' *Heracles* (*c.* 415 BCE) is the only other surviving ancient drama about Hercules' madness. At one time, criticism used to consist in discussing the differences between the Greek and Roman Hercules plays, typically to Seneca's discredit.[3] Euripidean drama is only one of many literary ingredients in Seneca's tragedy, however. Scholars now view Seneca's tragedies as Latin plays in a Roman tradition, and accordingly emphasize the play's interaction with the Augustan poets of the preceding generation. As Braden observes, the enduring value of the comparison with Euripides is to put Seneca's dramatic choices into sharper focus, a tactic that the preceding chapter employed to understand the problem of Hercules' madness.[4] Euripides' tragedy also responds to other contemporary tragedians, against whom he competed for a prize in a yearly Athenian dramatic festival. Our ability to trace the effects of such competition is limited by the fact that only fourteen tragedies written by other playwrights, those of Aeschylus and Sophocles, survive intact from the hundreds performed in Athens during the fifth and fourth centuries BCE. Euripides' conceptual and thematic points of reference derive from an intellectual tradition that ranges from Homer's epics to contemporary medical literature.

In Euripides' version, Heracles' shift into madness likely came as a dramatic surprise. Euripides' audience may not have expected his Heracles to kill his family at this point in his heroic career. The playwright may have invented the narrative where the hero's Labors precede the infanticide, and accordingly created some of the surprise by deviating from the standard mythological chronology. A mythographical handbook attributed to the second-century BCE scholar Apollodorus presents the opposite narrative, in which the Labors serve as expiation for the crime of killing his family. This mythographer likely drew on a pre-Euripidean version.[5] Seneca obviates this surprise through a prologue in which Juno lays out her plans to take revenge on Hercules. Euripides' play opens instead with the tyrant Lycus threatening Heracles' family, and so leaves the descent into madness as an unexpected plot twist.

When Seneca's hero eventually returns from the Underworld, he tells his wife and father that "I must wait to hold you in my arms" (638–9) and immediately rushes off to kill Lycus. Euripides' Heracles instead has a lengthy conversation with his wife and father (*Heracles* 514–636), then goes into the house to worship the gods while Amphitryon lures the king inside (701–25). Euripides gives his Heracles a long time on stage before the murders to establish his character as loving, reflective, and respectful. He embraces his children, consoles his terrified family, and remembers his obligations to the gods. This image of a protective Heracles recalls *Alcestis*, an earlier tragedy by Euripides in which the hero plays a minor role. In this play, Heracles again descends to the Underworld, this time not to remove Cerberus but to wrestle Death in order to bring back the heroine Alcestis and reunite her with her husband, king Admetus of Thessaly. In addition to fulfilling his traditional role as "averter of evil" (*alexikakos*), Heracles incidentally teaches the king how to behave toward his guests. The Heracles who first appears on stage in Euripides' *Heracles* as a sane, loving son and husband is similarly a fully humanized hero, able to perform incredible deeds of strength and heroism and yet also be part of a family. These sympathetic qualities make his transformation into a murderous madman even more pitiful and terrifying.

While the Chorus rejoice at their liberation from the tyrant, two goddesses appear above the stage on a crane called the *mechane*: Iris, Hera's messenger, and Lussa, the personification of madness. Their roles in Heracles' story are probably Euripides' invention as well.[6] Iris persuades a reluctant Lussa to drive Heracles mad at Hera's command (*Heracles* 815–74). Lussa protests that Heracles is a good man who has restored the gods' worship (849–54), and so she is fulfilling Hera's command against her own will (858). Yet soon afterwards, the goddess attacks Heracles, who then kills his own family under the delusion that he is killing Eurystheus and his family (922–1015). Seneca's Hercules has extravagant visions of entering Olympus, but Euripides gives his character more mundane hallucinations. He wrestles with an imaginary opponent and believes that he is besieging Eurystheus' city of Mycenae. The appearance of Lussa leaves interpreters of Euripides' play in no doubt as to the source of Heracles' madness. Seneca's play, by contrast, allows for greater ambiguity and psychological depth.

The denouement of Euripides' play sets Heracles in a different conflict with his father Amphitryon and friend Theseus. Once

Amphitryon has informed him of his crime, Heracles covers his face with a veil. At Theseus' entreaty, he unveils himself, but then announces his plan to die. As Wyles observes: "the Euripidean Heracles responds to crisis by withdrawal and has to be coaxed into action, while the Senecan hero responds by action (or intended action) and has to be restrained from it."[7] Theseus' effort to persuade Heracles to come to Athens occupies a much larger part of Euripides' final act, and characterizes him more fully as the man who remembered his gratitude to his friend and benefactor. In thanks for his rescue from the Underworld, he offers Heracles land and honor in his native city:

> For the law's sake, then, leave Thebes and come with me to the citadel of Pallas Athena. There I shall cleanse your hands from this taint and give you a home and a portion of my wealth ... All about the country allotments of land have been given to me. Mortals will henceforth call these yours for as long as you live. And when you die and go to the Underworld, the whole city of Athens will honor you with sacrifices and with massive temples of stone. For it will be a glorious achievement for the citizens in the eyes of Greece to win fair renown by doing good service to a noble hero. And this will also be my repayment to you for saving my life: for at present you stand in need of friends.
>
> Euripides, *Heracles* 1322–37, tr. Kovacs

For Athenian audiences, the city of Thebes occupied a different conceptual category in tragedy, as a dystopian "other" space that contrasted with their own idealized representations of their native city.[8] Theseus' praise of Athens as the city that sheltered Heracles and other exiles, such as Oedipus or the women taking refuge from the Theban civil war, establishes a patriotic contrast with the troubled city of Thebes and its corrupt monarchs.

The significant differences between Euripides' version of Hercules' madness and Seneca's are numerous. The scripts reflect responses to different dramatic and political situations. Euripides presented his play at a yearly Athenian civic festival, the City Dionysia, as part of a trilogy of tragedies performed with an extensive chorus and celebrity actors. Descriptions of music and dance indicating the characters' emotional states were likely reflected in shifts in the music played during the performance, in particular that of the *aulos,* a type of flute whose music was associated with the ecstatic worship of Dionysus.[9] The audiences that attended Euripides' plays were citizen-soldiers at war. A large percentage of Athenian citizen males served in a non-professional military and had experienced combat during Athens' many wars with other Greek city-states. The majority of the male, property-owning citizens could participate in the elections that chose the representatives who would declare these wars and the generals who would direct them. Their attendance at the tragedy was participation in a large-scale civic celebration as well as entertainment. The Athenian hero Theseus has a far more extensive role in Euripides' *Heracles,* as would be expected in a drama performed in Athens as part of a civic festival. The importance of his friendship with Heracles and the significance of his offer of shelter in Athens would accordingly be far greater for an Athenian audience. To listen to their local hero praise the virtues of gratitude and the excellence of their native city represented a moment of patriotism, one that Seneca truncates for his Roman audience. Theseus' friendship and hospitality, the contrast between Athens and Thebes, and perceptions of Heracles all had far different meanings for Euripides' Athenian audience than for Seneca's Romans.

Madness on stage between Euripides and Seneca

The extravagance of the representation of madness in Euripides' *Heracles* meant that it could easily be parodied. Euripides' contemporary, the comic poet Aristophanes, tells the story of how the mad Heracles drew his sword and fiercely attacked—not his own family, but an innkeeper who wanted him to pay for his food. In Aristophanes' comedy *Frogs* (405

BCE), the wine-god Dionysus dresses up as Heracles and endeavors to recreate the greatest of the hero's Labors. After consultation with Heracles himself, he descends to the Underworld not to carry off the monster Cerberus, but (in his initial plan) the recently deceased playwright Euripides. Once in the Underworld, the god's Heracles costume attracts the attention of an innkeeper and her maid, who accuse him of having taken all their food without paying on his last visit to the Underworld. Dionysus' slave Xanthias unconcernedly confirms their accusations, even though his master is only pretending to be Heracles:

Innkeeper: Plathane! Plathane, come here! Here's that hooligan, the one who came to the inn and gobbled sixteen loaves of bread! . . . Hah! You didn't think I'd recognize you again with those buskins on. Well? I haven't even mentioned all that fish yet.

Plathane: Right, dearie, or the fresh cheese that he ate up, baskets and all.

Innkeeper: And when I presented the bill, he gave me a nasty look and started bellowing.

Xanthias: That's his style exactly; he acts that way everywhere.

Innkeeper: And he drew his sword like a lunatic.

Plathane: Amen, my poor dear.

Innkeeper: And we were so scared I guess we jumped right up to the loft, while he dashed out and got away, taking our mattresses with him.

Xanthias: That's his style, too.

Aristophanes, *Frogs* 549–68, tr. Henderson

Passages such as these reflect the fact that Heracles was actually better known on the Athenian comic stage as a glutton and occasional madman than as a suffering hero on the tragic stage.[10] Approximately fifty years after Aristophanes' *Frogs*, images of Heracles' madness begin to appear on vases from South Italy. The best known of these images is by the painter Asteas from Paestum in south Italy, who depicted Heracles in the midst of killing his family on a vase now kept in Madrid (*c.* 350 BCE; see Fig. 1).[11]

Fig. 1 The madness of Heracles. Calyx krater signed by Asteas, *c.* 350 BCE.
Museo Arqueológico Nacional, Madrid, Spain. Inventory #11094.

Pache describes the scene as follows:

Herakles, carrying a small child in his arm, stands in the center. He turns toward an improvised pyre—a burning pile of furniture—on the left. Megara, on the right, watches the scene in terror, holding her left hand to her chest and her right to her head, in a gesture that denotes both panic and mourning. His nephew, Iolaos, and his mother, white-haired Alkmene, watch Herakles from a balcony above. Mania, to the left of Iolaos, also watches the scene from the balcony. All the characters' names are inscribed except for the child's.[12]

As Pache and Taplin observe, the scene does not reflect Euripides' *Heracles* but a different version of the story, perhaps one composed before Euripides' play. Euripides' Heracles murders his children by shooting them with arrows rather than hurling them into the fire, and Heracles' mother Alcmene and nephew Iolaus are not characters in this tragedy. Pache associates the narrative with Pherecydes of Athens, who lived in the first half of the fifth century BCE. A fragment of his genealogical work (no longer extant) indicates that Heracles killed his children by throwing them in the fire.[13] Asteas' depiction of Heracles' costume is also noteworthy, in that it does not include his lionskin and club, the attributes that enable the hero to be instantly recognized. Wyles speculates that the playwright of the unknown play on which this image is based may have "expressed Heracles' loss of identity and madness in this play through the exclusion of the hero's famous attributes."[14] Both Euripides and Seneca dramatize the slaves' removal of the weapons when Hercules collapses in a stupor after killing his family. Hercules' entreaties to regain them upon awakening so he can commit suicide suggest their intrinsic connection to his identity as a warrior.

Some of the symptoms of Heracles' madness resemble an epileptic fit. As the Messenger in Euripides' version indicates in relating the killing of the family to the Chorus, "his looks were utterly changed: his face was distorted with the agitation of his eyes, and in these blood-red streaks appeared, while foam dripped onto his handsome beard" (Euripides *Heracles* 933–5). Some contemporary Greek doctors called the condition we now recognize as epilepsy "the sacred disease," as they believed it was caused by possession by a divine power. The unknown author of a treatise entitled *On the Sacred Disease*, erroneously attributed in antiquity to Hippocrates, argued that the disease had mundane rather than divine causes. His description of the symptoms, however, show that both he and Euripides were likely envisioning the same condition: "the patient becomes speechless and chokes; froth flows from the mouth; he gnashes his teeth and twists his hands; the eyes roll and intelligence fails, and in some cases excrement is discharged" ([Hippocrates] *On the Sacred Disease* 10, tr. Jones).

Some Hellenistic scholars drew a more concrete association between epilepsy and Hercules' madness. The author of the pseudo-Aristotelian *Problems* (fourth–second century BCE) described epilepsy as a "Herculean disease," an idea that would become extremely popular in the Renaissance (see Chapter 5, p. 103). The author attributes both Hercules' excellence and his madness to an excess of black bile (*melancholia*) in his body:

> Why is it that all those men who have become extraordinary in philosophy, politics, poetry, or the arts are obviously melancholic, and some to such an extent that they are seized by the illnesses that come from black bile, as is said in connection with the stories about Heracles among heroes? Indeed, he seems to have been of this nature, and this is why the ancients named the illnesses of epilepsy "sacred disease" after him. And his insanity regarding his children and the eruption of sores that occurred before his disappearance on Mount Oeta prove this; for in many cases this occurs as a result of black bile.
>
> Pseudo-Aristotle, *Problems* 953a, tr. Mayhew and Mirhady

In Seneca's *Hercules Furens*, emphasis falls on Hercules' hallucinations, violent actions, and the stupor that follows. Before Hercules begins to kill the children, Amphitryon asks him, "Son, why are you frowning and shaking your face to and fro, / why do you strain your eyes to see an illusory sky?" (953–4). Amphitryon's order to Hercules to stop his insane behavior because his "great, heroic mind has fallen sick" (974) may reflect the connection between melancholia and greatness discussed in the pseudo-Aristotelian *Problems*. The playwright curtails the traditional account of physical symptoms of madness such as changing color or foaming at the mouth. Seneca's interest in the concluding Act is in Hercules' self-recognition and response to his guilt. His characters accordingly offer far lengthier descriptions of Hercules' stupor after his episode of violence and its moral significance.

These "Herculean" symptoms became a convention for the comic stage as well as the tragic. The Roman playwright Plautus (*c.* 250–180s BCE) employed them in his comedy *The Two Menaechmuses*, the original "comedy of errors" in which identical twins separated at birth become mistaken for one another. One of the Menaechmus twins, who goes by the name of Sosicles, travels one day from Syracuse to Epidamnus where unbeknownst to him, his twin brother lives. Sosicles reacts with surprise and suspicion when his brother's wife encounters him and assumes that he is in fact her husband because of their identical appearance. Each party thinks the other is mad: Sosicles has never seen his brother's wife before in his life, while she thinks his denials are yet further examples of his bad behavior in their terrible marriage. As often in Roman comedy, Sosicles parodically transforms himself into the madman that his brother's wife accuses him of being. The wife's description of Sosicles' pretended symptoms to her father play with the conventions of representing madness that begin with Euripides' Heracles:

> *Wife*: (*to her father*) Can you see how green his eyes are? How a pale color is arising from his temples and his forehead, how his eyes are flaming, look!
> *Sosicles*: (*aside*) Dear me! They say I am mad, when on the contrary they themselves are. Since they say that I'm mad, what's better for

> me than to pretend to be mad in order to drive them away from
> me? (*moves and acts strangely*)
> *Wife:* How he's gaping with a grimace! What should I do now, my dear
> father?
> *Wife's Father:* Come over here, my daughter, as far away from him as
> possible.
>
> Plautus, *The Two Menaechmuses* 829–34, 843, tr. de Melo

Euripides had also introduced other means of representing madness
on the stage that became conventions for later playwrights. As he runs
around the palace during his hallucination, Heracles believes that he is
traveling around Greece. As the Messenger reports, he claims to stop
at the city of Megara, the Isthmus of Corinth where he wrestles an
imaginary opponent in the Isthmian Games, and ends his hallucinatory
tour at Eurystheus' palace in Mycene (*Heracles* 953–63). The brief
moment during which Heracles participates in a fantasy wrestling
match shows Euripides' talent for mixing horror with humor. Yet
any humorous aspects of the episode immediately end as he begins
to kill his own children in the belief that they are Eurystheus's children.
The hallucinatory tour became a convention for later playwrights.
In *The Merchant*, another comedy by Plautus, the young lover
Charinus resolves to go into exile because his father has forbidden him
to see his girlfriend. Charinus similarly pretends to be insane and his
friend Eutychus tries to talk him down. In Plautus's version,[15] Charinus'
madness takes the form of traveling around the Mediterranean in
his mind:

> *Charinus:* I've already mounted my chariot, I've already taken the reins
> into my hands. (*pretends to be driving a chariot*)
> *Eutychus:* You're not in your right mind.
> *Charinus:* My feet, why won't you start running, directly to Cyprus,
> since my father is imposing exile on me?
> *Eutychus:* You're stupid. Please don't say that . . .
> *Charinus:* I've come to Cyprus now.

Eutychus: Do follow me so that you may see the girl you seek.

Charinus: I've made inquiries, but I haven't found her . . . I'm setting out to seek her further. Now I've arrived in Chalcis; there I can see a friend from Zacynthus. I tell him why I've come there; I ask if he's heard there who brought her, who has her.

Eutychus: Why won't you stop that nonsense and come in here with me?

Plautus, *The Merchant* 931–42, tr. de Melo

Plautus's comedies demonstrate that the madness of Hercules was established in Roman tradition two centuries before Seneca's tragedy, and well enough known that it could be parodied.

In Seneca, Amphitryon hopes that the sleep will heal his son (1050–2). The Chorus pray to personified Sleep to effect this healing (1066–81), even as they describe how the unconscious Hercules thrashes uneasily (1082–91). As is typical of this Chorus, they quickly move to interpreting Hercules' sleep in moral rather than in physical terms (1092–9). They hope that his sleep will enable his "heroic sense of duty" to return and take the place of madness. If it cannot, then they want his mind to remain "pure" by staying mad so he will not recognize himself as the perpetrator of his crimes and succumb to guilt, as Hercules will in fact do soon after at the beginning of Act 5. The Chorus do not yet realize what Hercules' contemplation and eventual dismissal of suicide in Act 5 will reveal: that his heroism consists in endurance, in living on despite his guilt rather than evading it in death. To remain mad forever would be the same kind of evasion of responsibility. By granting a moral dimension to Hercules' stupor, Seneca turns the traditional representation of Hercules' madness to new purposes.

Augustan Hercules and new modes of heroism

A particular aesthetic pleasure for the educated Roman audience of Seneca's tragedies came from hearing the poetic language spoken by the characters. This aspect of Senecan tragedy is more difficult for a modern audience to appreciate, since it is one of many features of poetic language that is most easily lost in translation. The language of Senecan tragedy is densely allusive: even the briefest two- or three-word phrase can evoke a series of responses to the foundational works of Augustan poetry, including Virgil's *Aeneid*, Ovid's *Metamorphoses*, and Horace's *Odes*. The Augustan epics present influential versions of the angry Juno, jealous of Jupiter's adulteries and eager to punish the innocent victims of his rapes. Virgil and Ovid also present characters in the grip of madness. Throughout his tragedies, Seneca invites comparisons between his themes, situations, and use of language and those of his distinguished predecessors.

As observed above (p. 42ff.), the opening speech of Seneca's *Hercules Furens* contrasts with Euripides' *Heracles*, which begins with a speech by the gentle Amphitryon. Juno's prolonged, furious complaint in Seneca's version instead addresses a Roman audience, who would immediately associate her with the angry goddess of Virgil's *Aeneid* and Ovid's *Metamorphoses*. The proem to the *Aeneid* describes the reasons for Juno's anger against the Trojans, which is similarly the result of her husband's infidelities:

> ... nor had her bitter resentment and the reasons for it ever left her mind. There still rankled deep in her heart the judgment of Paris and the injustice of the slight to her beauty, her loathing for the stock of Dardanus [an ancestor of the Trojan royal line] and her fury at the honors done to Ganymede, whom her husband Jupiter had carried off to be his cup-bearer. With all this fueling her anger she was keeping the remnants of the Trojans ... far away from Latium, driven by the Fates to wander year after year round all the oceans of the world.
>
> Virgil, *Aeneid* 1.25–32, tr. West

Juno's rage is a major theme of the *Aeneid*, recalled at significant moments throughout the poem. The narrator asks in the epic's proem: "Can there be such anger in the spirits of the heavenly gods?" (*Aeneid*

1.11, tr. West). Immediately after, he shows Juno ordering her servant Aeolus, king of the winds, to send a storm against the Trojan ships in an effort to wipe them out (*Aeneid* 1.50–156). The second half of the poem similarly opens with Juno working through a divine agent to harm Aeneas and his companions. This time her servant is the Fury Allecto, a demon from the Underworld charged with starting a war in Italy that Juno hopes will result in the extermination of the Trojans (*Aeneid* 7.286–571). In each episode, Juno expresses her concern that no one will respect her and worship her with sacrifices if she does not show her power to avenge perceived slights against her. In the poem's opening scene, she rages: "Who in the mean time worships Juno's divine power? What suppliant will place an offering on my altars?" (*Aeneid* 1.48–9). As the Trojans survive the hazardous journey from Troy and land in Italy in the poem's second half, Juno sarcastically reflects: "But I think my divine power at last lies exhausted, or I have satisfied my anger and I am at rest" (*Aeneid* 7.297–8). The poem ends with Juno promising to put her anger at the Trojans aside, in response to Jupiter's admonition that he will not tolerate further abuse (*Aeneid* 12.807–28). Yet this promise is only temporary, as she will harass Aeneas' descendants, the Roman people, in the Punic wars. For Virgil, Juno's anger presents Aeneas with the challenge of demonstrating his duty to his family, the people whom he leads, and the gods—in spite of their evident unfairness. The Romans called this sense of affectionate dutifulness *pietas*. Aeneas is the hero of *pietas* in part because he will not abandon his mission of resettling the Trojan people in Italy. Rather, he continues to the unknown, hostile land, not only braving the dangers but also rejecting the opportunities that he encounters to rest elsewhere and enjoy contentment. Juno's rage also serves a structural function for the organization of Virgil's epic. Her initial outburst sets the poem in motion, its reprise energizes its second half, and her apparent reconciliation provides one form of closure to the poem—though the poet does not narrate how the human characters reconcile their differences.

As a strong man, monster-slayer, and world traveler, Hercules was a desirable model for monarchic power. Some of his characteristic Greek cult titles, "savior" (*sôter*) and "averter of evil" (*alexikakos*), signified the conceptual work that he would do for Greek rulers long before the Roman emperors. As Hercules rid the earth of monsters and tyrants, turned back foreign invasions, and even faced down death itself, so too the ruler would terrify his enemies and keep his people safe. Alexander the Great began to mint coins featuring Hercules and Zeus soon after his accession to the throne.[16] According to the anecdotal tradition, he would dress in a lion skin and carry a club, a fashion adopted by his successors.[17] The Augustan poets could also represent Hercules in this tradition. Horace, Rome's preeminent lyric poet, describes how Jupiter's sons triumphed over their enemies and became gods themselves through their courage, integrity, and unyielding commitment. According to Horace, the emperor Augustus demonstrated similar qualities in the recent civil war and will follow in the gods' path after his death:

> The man of integrity who holds fast to his purpose is not shaken from his firm resolve by hot-headed citizens urging him to do wrong, or by the frown of an oppressive despot ... or by the mighty hand of thundering Jove. If the firmament were to split and crash down upon him, he will still be unafraid when hit by the wreckage. It was through this quality that Pollux and roving Hercules after a long struggle reached the fiery heights; reclining in their company, Augustus will drink nectar with rosy lips.
>
> Horace, *Odes* 3.3.1–12, tr. Rudd

In another poem in praise of Augustus, Horace imagines Roman farmers giving thanks to the emperor for protecting their lands from domestic and foreign enemies. In his dinnertime prayers, the householder makes offerings both to the emperor and to the *Lares*, domestic gods who guarantee the safety of his home and family. Horace compares the worship of the emperor by his Roman subjects to the

Greeks' worship of their divine protector Hercules: "He honors you [the emperor Augustus] with many prayers, pouring unmixed wine from dishes, and worship your divinity along with that of the household gods, just as Greece does in remembrance of Castor and great Hercules" (Horace *Odes* 4.5.33–6, tr. Rudd). Poems such as these foreground the emperor's role as a protector of his people who enjoys the favor of the gods, and turn to Hercules as a natural point of comparison.

A similar contrast with Hercules the savior helps to define the heroism of Aeneas as founder and man of duty.[18] Midway through the epic, Aeneas consults the Sibyl, an oracular priestess, to learn how to descend to the Underworld and return alive. He argues that he should be allowed to make the journey, like the heroes Orpheus, Theseus, and Hercules, because he too is descended from the gods (*Aeneid* 6.119–23). The Sibyl describes the journey in Herculean terms, as an "insane labor" (*Aeneid* 6.135). She sends Aeneas to complete the preliminary quest of retrieving the Golden Bough, a magical token that only comes to a man whom "the Fates call" (*Aeneid* 6.147) to travel to the Underworld. Charon, the ferryman of the dead, challenges Aeneas as he attempts to cross the river Styx and complains that the other heroic visitors only came in order to steal, whether Persephone (Theseus) or Cerberus (Hercules) (*Aeneid* 6.384–97). The Sibyl displays the Golden Bough to persuade Charon (and the reader) that Aeneas is a morally superior hero to Hercules. Aeneas descends to the Underworld at his father's request (*Aeneid* 5.724–39) not to steal but rather to learn about the future of the Roman people who will descend from him. The hero speaks with his dead father Anchises in order to better lead the Trojans who follow him toward their destiny. This exploit exemplifies Aeneas' characteristic virtue of *pietas*. His visit to the Underworld provides comfort to his father's lonely ghost; he serves his people by learning their future; and the Golden Bough indicates that his journey fulfills the commands of fate. The heroism of Aeneas's journey consists in his fulfillment of his obligations to his family, nation, and gods.

Near the end of the Underworld episode, Virgil presents a traditional comparison between Hercules and Augustus, Rome's first emperor, who claimed to be a descendant of Aeneas. As Anchises lists the Romans who will be born from Aeneas, he praises the emperor Augustus as a greater world conqueror than Hercules: "Hercules himself did not make his way to so many lands, though his arrow pierced the hind with hooves of bronze, though he gave peace to Erymanthus and made Lerna tremble at his bow" (*Aeneid* 6.801–3, tr. West). In Anchises' panegyric, which reflects Augustus' own propaganda, the emperor will offer Rome the secure peace of a new Golden Age. His rule will extend throughout the whole world, even beyond the Indians. By implication, Hercules is an inferior hero: he only killed monsters rather than bringing about peace between men, and did not rule over the territories he visited (see Chapter 4, p. 87ff.).

Soon after Aeneas returns to the world above, Hercules also becomes as an exemplary model for him. Juno instigates war between Aeneas's Trojans and the local Italians. In the hope of recruiting allies, he visits the Arcadian king Evander, whose people have settled on the site that will one day become the city of Rome. Evander tells his guest the story of how Hercules killed the monster Cacus, who dwelled in a nearby cave, and enabled the Arcadians to settle in peace. In Greek, the names *Evander* and *Cacus* mean "Good Man" and "Bad Man" respectively: this is about as simple as an allegorical story can get. The Arcadians are poor and live in an unimpressive city, though the Roman reader knows the site has a glorious future. Evander urges his guest not to confuse their poverty for insignificance, as he will be following in the footsteps of Hercules if he accepts his hospitality:

> The victorious Hercules of the line of Alceus stooped to enter this door. This was a palace large enough for him. You are my guest, and you too must have the courage to despise wealth. You must mould yourself to be worthy of the god. Come into my poor home and do not judge it too harshly.
>
> Virgil, *Aeneid* 8.362–5, tr. West

The remainder of the poem shows some of the aspects of Aeneas's "moulding" himself in the image of the god. Hercules' killing of the monster Cacus enabled the Arcadians to found their city. Aeneas also fights a war in Italy so his Trojan people can settle after their long wanderings. Yet, as Putnam has observed, there remain unavoidable similarities between Virgil's hero Hercules and monster Cacus. Both are arrogant and prone to rage, and both use violence as a first response. Putnam concludes: "the twining of Cacus and Hercules by means of pride and anger questions not only the quality of Hercules' immediate mission but also any easy linkage between Hercules and future Roman political genius, especially if such a bond is meant to assert a sense of moral superiority."[19] The violence of Aeneas's war forever disrupts life in Latium. Compensation, if it can be called that, only comes centuries later with the rise of the Roman empire. The analogy with Hercules does clarify that the changes brought by heroes are rarely universal benefits: their exploits always create winners and losers. A different contrast between Aeneas and Hercules comes in the sequel to their exploits. The Trojan exile stays in Latium to found a city and marry a Latin bride, but the wandering Greek hero does not get to enjoy any immediate benefit of comfort or security from his Labors. As Hercules' family and the Chorus observe in Seneca's tragedy, no sooner does he complete one than he dashes off to undertake another. Arrival in Italy and victory in war similarly does not grant Aeneas safety or comfort, as Jupiter foretells at the beginning of the poem that he will die within a few years of the war's completion (*Aeneid* 1.265–6). The divinization and celebration of both heroes constitute their most meaningful recompense for their labors.

The figure of the angry Juno, resolved to punish innocent victims because of her anger at her husband Jupiter, recurs in Ovid's *Metamorphoses*, an epic written in the generation after the *Aeneid*. Ovid varies, develops, and questions Virgil's presentation of divine anger and its consequences. In Ovid's epic, Juno's interventions lead to devastation in Thebes and elsewhere. She attacks Jupiter's numerous rape victims, including Callisto, Semele, Alcmena, and others.[20] In the Semele episode, Ovid's Juno announces her revenge in terms that recall the *Aeneid*: "I must destroy her, if I am fittingly called greatest Juno ... if I am queen and sister and wife of Jupiter—certainly his sister" (Ovid *Metamorphoses* 3.263–6). The revenge worked by Ovid's Juno is incomplete, however: she is able to destroy Semele but not Bacchus, Semele's son by Jupiter. Like Jupiter's other illegitimate son Hercules, Bacchus soon ascends to heaven and becomes a god. In the following book of the *Metamorphoses*, Juno grows offended at Semele's sister Ino for her worship of Bacchus as a god. "Can Juno do nothing except lament unavenged grief?" (*Metamorphoses* 4.426). She sends the Fury Tisiphone to drive both Ino and her husband Athamas mad. He immediately slaughters one of his sons, and Ino in her madness leaps into the sea with her other son, where Venus takes pity on her and asks Neptune to transform mother and child into sea gods (*Metamorphoses* 4.464–542). Ovid's Juno causes families to degenerate into madness and commit violence against one another. Virgil left this hideous form of vengeance unexplored; Ovid outdoes his epic predecessor in terms of the cruelty he can ascribe to Juno.

Hinds emphasizes the degree to which the mythological world that Seneca's characters inhabit is an Ovidian one. Thebes becomes a particularly Ovidian site for Latin poets writing after the Augustan period, as Ovid had devoted books 3 and 4 of his *Metamorphoses* to telling episodes of Theban legend. In addition, the first Chorus of *Hercules Furens* recalls the stories of Pentheus and Procne. For us, Euripides' *Bacchae* is the most famous version of the Pentheus story, while Seneca likely also had access to Sophocles' *Tereus,* a tragedy no longer extant, for the Procne and Philomela story. Greek tragedy, however, was likely not the primary version of these stories for Seneca's Roman audience, as Ovid had told both stories at length in the *Metamorphoses*.[21] In Hinds' words, the Chorus of Seneca's *Oedipus*, another drama that takes place in Thebes "sets Oedipus in the context of a markedly Ovidian version of the mythology of the Cadmean Thebes."[22] After Ovid, Thebes takes on the role of conceptual alternative to Rome, a dystopian "other" space where Romans could work through their anxieties about their city.

Seneca's post-Augustan hero

Seneca's Hercules recalls Virgil's Aeneas in his endurance of persecution by Juno, but otherwise exemplifies a much narrower array of moral qualities. Where Aeneas is concerned to serve his family, people, and gods, Hercules is a fundamentally self-interested hero. The Chorus observe that he performs his Labors in order to increase his glory, and Amphitryon and Megara lament that Hercules has little choice in the matter thanks to his enslavement by Eurystheus. As observed in Chapter 2 (p. 22ff.), the characters are interested in defining the hero's *virtus*. Only once, however, do they ascribe dutifulness (*pietas*) hypothetically to him, when the Chorus pray that his "heroic sense of duty" will return after his sleep (1093). The contrast with the other-directed virtues of a hero like Aeneas suggests much of the dissatisfaction with *Hercules Furens* expressed by the previous generation of critics. Hercules' self-aggrandizing language and action led earlier critics to label him as a victim of hubris, whose "moral feebleness" appears "ludicrous," and whose "overreaching caused his tragedy."[23] As argued in the previous chapters, Seneca uses the figure of Hercules not to investigate the cooperative virtues but the quality of endurance.

Some of Hercules' monster-slaying and landscape-altering Labors benefit ordinary human beings who now enjoy a safer environment. That can hardly be said about the removal of Cerberus from the Underworld, however, as Hercules' conquest of death does not empower others to do the same. The hero's behavior in the Underworld instead confirms the negative impression that Virgil's narrator and characters had of Hercules. Seneca's Hercules becomes the vandal that Virgil's Charon remembered: he seizes the ferryman's pole and beats him with it (773–5). Though Juno's assault on Hercules may be excessive, his violent behavior in the world below legitimates her exhortation to the Furies to "take your revenge for Hades' desecration!" (104). Virgil's Sibyl steers Aeneas carefully away from Underworld locations that might pose a threat to his moral integrity, such as Tartarus where the great sinners are punished, and instead guides him along the road to Elysium where the virtuous are rewarded (*Aeneid* 6.542–3). Seneca's Theseus, however, claims that he saw exactly those places that the hero of duty (*pietas*) was forbidden to see, and did so in the company of Hercules (737–9, 750–9). The implication derived from attention to Aeneas' journey is that both of the Senecan heroes have been tainted by their contact with the great sinners.

The play's final Act amplifies the contrast between Hercules' self-interest and Aeneas' other-directed virtue by showing the hero's interaction with his father. As mentioned above, Aeneas undertakes his journey to the Underworld not in hope of glory but in obedience to his father's request. Virgil's ghost of Anchises greets his son with praise of his fulfillment of one of the greatest challenges of *pietas*, risking death in order to be reunited (*Aeneid* 6.687–8). The final act of Seneca's tragedy shows an interaction between father and son that presents the Virgilian scene inverted. Like Anchises, Amphitryon is reunited with his son after a long absence, but finds him committing the worst possible act of undutifulness (*impietas*), killing his wife and children. Where Anchises delights in being reunited with his son, however briefly, Amphitryon instead must plead with Hercules not to kill himself and thus abandon his father again. When he returns to his senses and recognizes his crime, Hercules appeals to *pietas* in a different sense than either his father or Anchises understand it. He thinks that killing himself will exemplify *pietas* by allowing him to atone for his crime (1269). Only when Amphitryon threatens to kill himself first does Hercules finally realize that his father needs his support and companionship rather than his death. The play ends with Hercules recognizing that his father and friend need him to remain alive and employ his strength for the benefit of others.

Like Virgil's Juno, Seneca's goddess is visible at the beginning rather than an offstage presence like the Hera of Euripides' play. The extended length of Juno's opening monologue recalls a form frequently used in the epic genre, in which characters typically deliver speeches of comparable length. Seneca's Juno expands the briefer monologues of the epic Junos in expressing her rage against Aeneas and the Trojans. As Putnam observes, "the opening monologue of Juno ... carefully echoes the initial lines of the *Aeneid* with phraseology ... to such a degree that it often resembles a powerful dramatization, in soliloquy, of what Virgil leaves implicit in his third-person narrative."[24] The playwright clearly signals his recombination of the Virgilian and Ovidian traditions in the opening line of the play, which recalls the frustration of Ovid's Juno at Semele: "I am sister of the Thunderer-- only his sister" (1). The goddess's catalog of Jupiter's rape victims transformed into stars also recalls the *Metamorphoses* in its form, as Ovid's epic is a compendium of transformation myths where Virgil's poem focuses on one single major story. Seneca's Juno is determined to avenge herself on her unfaithful husband Jupiter by punishing his illegitimate child Hercules, and like both of her Augustan counterparts uses madness as her weapon. As discussed in Chapter 2 (p. 18ff.), some of the play's critics seek the explanation for Hercules' episode of madness in the earlier violence of the Labors. While this may make psychological sense to modern readers, it ignores the significance of the play's opening scene. Seneca's careful evocation of his Augustan predecessors would have left the Roman audience in little doubt that Juno can make good on her threat, which occupies the final third of her monologue (86–122), to summon the Furies to drive her victim mad.

Seneca created his Juno and Hercules as part of a new work that drew upon the Euripidean, Virgilian, and Ovidian traditions.[25] In one of his *Moral Letters,* Seneca explains how his compositional strategy is eclectic imitation rather than adaptation of a single major source. He compares his practice as a writer to the bees who collect nectar from various flowers and transform it into honey:[26]

> We also, I say, ought to copy these bees, and sift whatever we have gathered from a varied course of reading, for such things are better preserved if they are kept separate; then, by applying the supervising care with which our nature has endowed us,—in other words, our natural gifts,—we should so blend those several flavours into one delicious compound that, even though it betrays its origin, yet it nevertheless is clearly a different thing from that whence it came.
>
> Seneca, *Moral Letters* 84.5, tr. Gummere.

As for all of the classical Latin poets, creation means adaptation of the work of multiple predecessors. New works come not from thin air but from intense interaction with the preceding literary tradition. As in many modern art forms, from film to jazz, their strength derives in part from the reader's recognition of their dependence on the tradition, which the poet encourages rather than attempting to conceal. Seneca sets his works in direct competition with those of the greatest poets of the preceding generation. The poet of Hercules' Labors has no small ambitions.

4

Hercules Furens and Seneca's Career

Thanks in part to his roles as a prolific author and imperial courtier, Seneca's life is better documented than those of many writers from antiquity. His writing was popular in his own day, and its classic status would not be seriously questioned until the nineteenth century. Scholars assign Seneca's birth somewhere between 4 and 1 BCE in Corduba, the modern Córdoba in Spain. His father moved the family to Rome, where he became a prominent rhetorician. We possess two rhetoric collections from the Elder Seneca, *Declamations* (*Controversiae*) and *Persuasive Speeches* (*Suasoriae*). The *Declamations* are excerpts from practice speeches on a variety of themes, with comments by famous rhetoricians of the Elder Seneca's day. The *Persuasive Speeches* offer advice to characters from history and mythology at particular moments of crisis. *Persuasive Speech* 3, entitled "Agamemnon deliberates whether to sacrifice Iphigenia: for Calchas says that otherwise sailing is impermissible" (tr. Winterbottom), could easily have been part of a Senecan tragedy. Agamemnon, the commander of the Greek army, is about to sail to Troy, but finds that the winds will not blow. The prophet Calchas tells him that he has killed one of the goddess Artemis's sacred deer and so must sacrifice his daughter Iphigenia as restitution in order to get the wind he needs. The Elder Seneca recalls a series of declaimers from his own day who argued for and against the sacrifice, and discusses how some of them imitated phrases from Virgil. Agamemnon also appears in several Senecan dramas. In Seneca's *Agamemnon*, his wife Clytemnestra appeals to her husband's sacrifice of their daughter as a motive for killing him in revenge. Like the declamations, the lengthy speeches of Senecan tragedy show similar dramatizations of mythological situations, epigrammatic fireworks, and adaptation of Virgil and the other Augustan poets.

The earliest years of Seneca's career remain a mystery to us, and we must speculate from incomplete evidence about when he wrote many of his most famous works. In 39 CE, Seneca was evidently both a senator and an oratorical star, because the emperor Caligula wanted to put him to death out of jealousy, "merely because he pleaded a case well in the Senate while the emperor was present" (Cassius Dio, *Roman History* 59.19.7, tr. Cary). The emperor relented only because one of the women in his circle indicated Seneca was ill and would die soon. Soon after Caligula's assassination in 41 CE and Claudius' accession to the throne, the historian Cassius Dio (60.8.5) reports how Seneca again suffered from jealousy in the emperor's household. In the first year of his reign, Claudius exiled Seneca to Corsica on a charge of adultery with Julia Livilla, Caligula's sister. Dio attributes this exile to Claudius' wife Messalina's jealousy of Julia. Though the historian does not elaborate on Seneca's role in the scandal, it is nevertheless clear from this anecdote how far the courtier had left his Spanish provincial origins behind him.

During the eight years of his exile on Corsica, Seneca composed a number of philosophical essays and likely some of the early tragedies. Claudius' wife Agrippina took notice of his rhetorical skills, and recalled him in 50 CE to serve as tutor in rhetoric to her teenage son Nero. When Claudius died four years later in 54 CE and Nero succeeded to the throne, Seneca composed two works to assist his young student's movement into imperial power. These were Nero's inaugural speech, which no longer survives, and *Apocolocyntosis* ("Pumpkinification"), a satire mocking the deceased emperor Claudius as a coward and a buffoon.[1] In Tacitus' account of Nero's delivery of the inaugural speech that Seneca composed for him, the philosopher and playwright appears as "that famous man, whose pleasing talent was so well suited to a contemporary audience" (*Annals* 13.3).

Seneca continued to serve as an advisor and speechwriter for the first five years of Nero's reign (54–59 CE), during which time the emperor's rule was apparently just and moderate. The ancient sources refer to this period as "Nero's five years," in order to distinguish them from the emperor's later descent into tyranny. The emperor also enriched Seneca tremendously, making him one of the wealthiest men in Rome.[2] Later in Nero's reign, however, Seneca perceived that his influence over the emperor was declining and attempted to withdraw from the court. The emperor at first forbade him, but eventually permitted him to retire to his villa in 62 CE. Approaching 70 and never in good health, Seneca appears to have composed many of his philosophical essays and *Moral Letters* during this period, perhaps in an effort to secure his legacy for future generations. In 65 CE, Nero uncovered a conspiracy by members of the Roman nobility to assassinate him and replace him with the aristocrat Gaius Calpurnius Piso. Some of the participants in this conspiracy implicated Seneca. The emperor responded by sending soldiers to Seneca's villa to order him to commit suicide. Later ages would use his carefully orchestrated suicide to make him into a martyr who attractively showed future lovers of freedom how to oppose tyrants with self-possession and style.[3] Peter Paul Rubens' classic painting of "The Death of Seneca" (1614) (see Fig. 2) offers an influential example of the Renaissance cult of Seneca. Chapter 5 examines Seneca's immense popularity on the Renaissance stage through discussion of the plays of Shakespeare, Rubens' near-contemporary.

As with many literary works from antiquity, we cannot know for certain when Seneca wrote *Hercules Furens*. Its commentary on the exercise of power pertains easily to the reign of any absolute monarch, and its mythological narrative contains no specific references to datable historical events. Scholars accordingly look outside the playscript to the satire *Apocolocyntosis*, where Seneca appears to parody not only the emperor Claudius but this very tragedy. *Apocolocyntosis* could have

Fig. 2 Peter Paul Rubens, *The Death of Seneca* (1614).
Alte Pinakothek, Munich, Germany © PRISMA ARCHIVO / Alamy Stock Photo.

been performed at the Saturnalia festival in late December 54 CE, a few weeks after Claudius' death in October of the same year.[4] As the deceased emperor seeks admission into Olympus, Hercules questions him in his role as heaven's gatekeeper. "To make himself more awe-inspiring," Seneca's narrator observes, Hercules "became a tragic character" (*Apocolocyntosis* 7, tr. Nussbaum).[5] Hercules' speech is in the meter of tragic dialogue, a six-beat line called the iambic *senarius*, and his boasts appear similar to those uttered by the character of Seneca's tragedy: "Oft has this cudgel slain ferocious kings!" Seneca's purpose is deride the emperor who exiled him, however, and so he makes the emperor Augustus rebuke Claudius as the murderer of many members of the Julio-Claudian family. The god Mercury then leads Claudius down to the Underworld. As they pass through Rome, they see a crowd chanting his funeral song in anapaestic meter (*Apocolocyntosis* 12). This poetic meter is familiar from the choruses of Senecan tragedy, including *Hercules Furens'* first and final choral odes (see Chapter 1, p. 3ff). If we accept the traditional, though speculative dating of both the tragedy and the satire that appears to parody it, then Seneca in fact wrote much of the work that survives to us after *Hercules Furens*. These works include the majority of the tragedies, some of his most important philosophical essays, and the lengthy *Moral Letters*. Yet tracing the connections between this play and the rest of his corpus does not show an evolution in thought so much as the presentation of familiar motifs and ideas in new and different contexts.

Seneca the tragedian

The only Roman tragedies that survive in full versions rather than in fragments quoted in other authors are Seneca's eight genuine plays and two others traditionally, though incorrectly attributed to him.[6] Roman tragedy, however, was a vibrant art form before Seneca's time. Roman authors' quotations and reminiscences show us the popularity of the originators of the form, Quintus Ennius, Marcus Pacuvius, and Lucius Accius. Varius' *Thyestes* and Ovid's *Medea* were some of the most popular tragedies of the Augustan era by two of its foremost poets.[7] Members of the Roman aristocracy also wrote tragedies as diversions. The emperor Augustus wrote an *Ajax*, for example, but was unsatisfied with it. He destroyed it and told his friends that his suicidal hero had "fallen on his sponge" (Suetonius *Augustus* 85.2), the ancient equivalent of an eraser. In Seneca's generation, Pomponius Secundus also wrote tragedies and apparently argued with Seneca about diction.[8]

One of Seneca's most distinctive legacies to Western theatre is the figure of the revenger, which Renaissance playwrights would develop into a popular character type (see Chapter 5). Juno's lengthy opening monologue presents many of the typical characteristics of Senecan revenge. Her hatred of her enemy "will never end"; in her words, "my passionate heart / will whip up everlasting anger" (27–8). She claims that her need for revenge has also driven her insane, and so the revenge she inflicts on her enemy makes him similar to herself. She addresses the Furies whom she will send to attack Hercules with madness:

> To capture Hercules' mind, to whip him up
> to desperate, passionate madness, you must first
> go mad yourselves. —Juno, why so calm?
> Sisters, let me be the first flung from my mind;
> turn me upside-down and make me ready
> to do what a stepmother should.
>
> Seneca, *Hercules Furens* 107–12

The Senecan revengers of the other plays may be human, but they are no less figures of hatred and madness. Medea prepares herself to take revenge on her faithless husband Jason by commanding herself to "take on the armor of anger, prepare for destruction / possessed by fury" (*Medea* 51–2). At the beginning of *Thyestes*, the Fury spurs on the ghost of Tantalus to drive his grandson Atreus mad. The transmission of madness once more creates a resemblance between the attacker and the victim. As the Fury orders the ghost: "Spread your madness through the house. / Make them [Tantalus' grandsons Atreus and Thyestes] resemble you, make them hate, make them thirst / to drink their own blood" (*Thyestes* 101–3). Atreus is the paradigmatic Senecan revenger, eager to destroy the brother who usurped his throne and slept with his wife. As their grandfather Tantalus killed his own child and served him as a meal to the gods, so Atreus will make his brother Thyestes consume his own children. Like Juno, he knows ordinary retaliation such as murder will not satisfy his need for revenge, and so he dreams up a stratagem that will turn his victim against himself.

In the prologue to *Hercules Furens,* Juno realizes that the monsters she has flung against Hercules are insufficient. For him to face a worthy opponent, "there is none but himself. So let him fight himself" (85). The sense that something greater is coming sets the audience looking both forward to see how their dramatic expectations will be fulfilled, and backward to the previous literary tradition. Other Senecan characters typically view their narratives as something "greater than" what has occurred, either in others' stories or their own. Thus as Atreus deliberates on how best to punish his brother, he comments "my heart is swollen with some greater thing, / something extraordinary, more than human" (*Thyestes* 267–8). He then claims to derive his idea of killing and serving his brother's children from Procne, the Athenian princess who took similar revenge on her husband Tereus after he raped her sister Philomela. The Senecan revengers exhibit a characteristic (and thoroughly non-naturalistic) self-consciousness in the speeches planning their vengeance. At the beginning of *Medea* Act 4, the Nurse uses the "greater than" theme to contrast Medea's upcoming murder of the children with the witch's prior feats: "I have often seen her in her rages, attacking the gods, / bringing down the sky. But horrors, greater horrors, / Medea plans" (*Medea* 673–5). Though the Nurse is as yet unaware of Medea's plan, the audience knows that this is the crime through which she will "become" Medea.

The goddess Juno in *Hercules Furens* has none to oppose her, but in other plays Seneca uses dialogue between the revenger and a lesser character to explore the elliptical logic of the revenger's madness. In *Thyestes,* Atreus' servant tries unsuccessfully to dissuade his master from undertaking extravagant revenge on his brother. In the servant's view, Atreus should think of the people's likely reaction if their king commits murder. He should ensure the security of his kingdom through trust and good actions, and he should remember that it is wrong to kill his brother, even if his brother wronged him first (*Thyestes* 204–19). The servant's arguments reflect conventional morality, and have no effect on the tyrant who inhabits a completely different moral universe. Power for Atreus means domination; he aims to control the people through fear rather than win their love. For him, "any wrong is right against a brother like that" (*Thyestes* 220), a sentiment likely shared by his brother. Lycus of *Hercules Furens* appears like an insecure moderate in comparison to this thoroughly self-sufficient monster. He initially seeks to ingratiate himself with his people by marrying Megara, and expresses his anxieties by denigrating Hercules as a mere mortal rather than proudly proclaiming that he can defeat any opponent.

Other "passion-restraint" type-scenes such as *Thyestes* Act 2 include *Phaedra* Act 1, in which the heroine reveals to her Nurse that she has conceived an incestuous passion for her stepson Hippolytus. Like Atreus' servant, the Nurse gives her mistress common-sense advice, urging her to avoid incest and love her husband Theseus instead. As with Atreus's madness, Phaedra's passion is the result of an inherited curse and so she cannot choose to stop even as she knows she is making a terrible mistake. In support of the restraining characters, the Senecan choruses often present arguments for moderation.[9] Thus the Chorus of *Thyestes* (344–403) makes a Stoic-inflected argument that true kingship is not about wealth and ambition, but accepting fate (even death) willingly, while the Chorus of *Phaedra* (1123–40) observes that Fortune strikes the powerful more severely than the weak. Like the first Chorus of *Hercules Furens*, which alludes to Euripides' *Phaethon* (see Chapter 2, p. 35ff.), the Chorus of *Oedipus* (882–910) uses another mythological contrast with an ambitious young man in its argument for moderation. They prefer an unexciting voyage down "the middle path" (891) of life rather than crashing from heaven like Icarus, who fell from the sky when he flew too close to the sun. In *Hercules Furens*, the passion-restraint type-scene occurs in Act 5, where Amphitryon and Theseus successfully talk Hercules down from suicide. In the other tragedies, the effort to restrain the protagonist takes place before the protagonist commits the central action of the play, and is typically unsuccessful. By locating a successful "passion-restraint" scene in the denouement of *Hercules Furens*, Seneca shows that the action of the play that requires significant negotiation is not Hercules' assault on his family but his eventual decision to live on.

Senecan characters display an enhanced self-awareness that is entirely non-naturalistic. They regard a particular set of characteristic actions and traits, determined by the prior mythological tradition, as essential to their identities. Most famously, Medea asserts to her Nurse that she will "become Medea" by committing the revenge that the audience is waiting for her to perform, and proudly announces "now I am Medea" as she prepares to kill her children (*Medea* 171, 910). In a rhetorical move that modern readers typically find artificial, Senecan characters often address themselves in an effort to call themselves up to their own perceived standards, which are in fact those of the tradition. Thus when Ulysses in *Trojan Women* must figure out where Andromache has hidden her son Astyanax, he appeals to the characteristic cunning that makes him Ulysses: "Now, my mind, it is time to summon up your cunning; time for deceit and fraud, time to be all Ulysses" (*Trojan Women* 613–14). For Hercules, the Labors have come to form the paradigm of his existence, and so he regards each new challenge as one of an endless series of Labors. When he plans to commit suicide upon realizing his guilt, he describes it as the next Labor: "Come, right hand, / try a mighty labor, bigger than the Twelve. / Coward, why do you hesitate?" (1281–3). Hercules' view does not change once his father has persuaded him to stay alive: "Let this Labor now be added to my Labors: / staying alive" (1316–17). Not to undertake new Labors eagerly and boldly would mean not being

Hercules, just as not to take revenge would mean not being Medea or not to be cunning would mean not being Ulysses.

Scholars have recently focused on how Seneca's characters appear to will themselves into creation through self-defining speeches. Identifying the constitutive elements of the self, or defining its uniqueness and its boundaries, no longer seems as straightforward a task in the post-modern era as it did in previous generations. Along with many other humanistic and scientific disciplines, classical scholars have renewed the inquiry into the nature of the self. Bartsch has discussed the contrast between the ideal self of the *Moral Letters*, who has attained self-cultivated perfection, and the "proficient" self whose "full-time occupation ... is the *pursuit* of the ideal."[10] Dramatic tension can arise from the tragic characters' efforts to become the image that the tradition has already created for them. As Gill has argued, second thoughts in Senecan drama can threaten a character's integrity.[11] If Medea succumbs to her maternal feelings and does not murder her children, in what sense will she still be Medea? Her address to herself is an attempt to reintegrate a self being torn apart by contradictory impulses: "Why, my soul, do you waver? ... Why am I led in two directions, now by anger, / now by love? My double inclination tears me apart" (*Medea* 937–9). Star has focused on the rhetorical aspect of these scenes of self-creation. In passages such as Medea's wavering and Hercules' address to his right hand (quoted in the preceding paragraph), the "creation and maintenance of a consistent self" is "based around the repetition of the figure of self-apostrophe [address to oneself] and command."[12]

Seneca's characters speak in a declamatory style that recalls the Elder Seneca's *Declamations* and *Persuasive Speeches*.[13] One characteristic aspect of Seneca's tragic rhetoric is the short statement of traditional wisdom that the Romans called a *sententia*. Lycus's observation on Realpolitik was a particular favorite for later ages: "the reasons for war do not matter; the main thing is its end". If you want to compose *sententiae*, Latin is a better language than English in which to do so, because Latin is much more compressed.[14] In Latin, Lycus speaks a five-word sentence: *quaeritur belli exitus, / non causa* (406–7). Latin verbs provide the information in a single word that English often separates into several different words. "It is looked for" is four words in English (subject pronoun, auxiliary verb, verb participle, and verbal complement), but one word in Latin: *quaeritur.* The inflected forms of Latin nouns often obviate the need for prepositions: "for war" is two words in English, but one word in Latin: *belli.* Latin also does not use the definite or indefinite articles "the" or "a" as English must. The effects of such linguistic compression usually cannot be rendered in English, and omission of the English article often sounds bizarre. That is why Wilson's translation appropriately substitutes a much lengthier sentence with a wholly different structure. As such, the incisive force of the *sententia* is one of the first aspects of Senecan rhetoric to be lost in translation. The English reader is left to read a piece of fortune-cookie wisdom, without the brevity, rhythm, and word order that originally made it memorable, and may conclude incautiously that Seneca was a conventional writer. Nothing could be further from the truth. Seneca himself attests to the power of *sententiae* in the theatre of his day: "Have you not noticed how the theatre reechoes whenever any words are spoken whose truth we appreciate generally and confirm unanimously?" (*Moral Letters* 108.8, tr. Gummere).[15] Not everyone, of course, shared this enthusiasm for the sententious style that aimed for epigrammatic high points and occasionally sacrificed logical development. The emperor Caligula criticized Seneca's style as "sand without lime" (Suetonius *Caligula* 53.2), or individual elements without a structure to bind them together.

Seneca the philosopher

As well as writing tragedies, Seneca was an extraordinarily prolific writer in a wide variety of genres. One scholar has recently called him

"Seneca *Multiplex.*"[16] Writing in the 90s CE, about twenty-five years after Seneca's death, Quintilian reports that "he put his hand to almost every type of literature. Speeches, poems, letters, and dialogues of his are in circulation" (*The Orator's Education* 10.1.129). The rhetoric teacher found that his students were eager readers of Seneca, seduced by a style that he perceived as decadent: "at that time Seneca was almost the only author in young men's hands . . . The young loved him more than they imitated him, and fell as far below him as he had fallen below the ancients" (10.1.126–7, tr. Russell). Seneca also wrote a series of scientific works, only one of which survives to us, the *Questions About Nature* in seven books. Other authors attest that he wrote studies of fish, stones, earthquakes, and ethnographies of India and Egypt.

When writing natural philosophy, Seneca describes the world's physical changes in a rationalizing mode that differs considerably from the tragedies' mythological mode. For example, Megara proudly describes how her husband Hercules split open the Tempe pass (*HF* 284–8; see p. 37). As early as the fifth century BCE, however, Greek authors proposed a rationalizing account. The Greek historian Herodotus attributed the opening of the pass to an earthquake that separated the mountains Pelion and Ossa (*Histories* 7.129). For Seneca, earthquakes such as this one, as well as more recent ones that devastated Pompeii in 62 CE (some years before the more famous volcanic eruption), occur because of a mass of air trapped under the earth:

> When moving air with great force completely fills an empty space under the earth and proceeds to struggle and think about a way out it repeatedly strikes the side-walls within which it lurks, over which cities are sometimes situated. These "walls" are sometimes so shaken that buildings placed above them fall down, sometimes to such an extent that the walls which support the whole covering of the cave fall into the vacant space underground and entire cities collapse into the immense depths.
>
> Seneca, *Questions About Nature* 6.25.1

Seneca's account of the reasons for seismic activity differ from current understanding, as the theory of plate tectonics would not be elaborated until the twentieth century. Yet neither does it require appeal to mythological forces. The point of this argument, as with many other Senecan scientific writings, is to assert that the world can be understood and to diminish fear of the unknown.[17] As Williams observes, Seneca attributes "a complete grasp of nature and his fearless superiority over all that she throws against him" to the wise person. "Such a man embodies the Lucretian/Senecan sublimity of thought that transports the mind beyond conventional human vulnerability."[18] Natural disasters may be threatening, but the wise reader will know that they occur as the result of explicable natural forces rather than for fantastic reasons such as the malevolence of the gods or the efforts of a heroic strongman.

Many of Seneca's philosophical works involve episodes of dialogue in which the narrator attributes positions to an imaginary interlocutor and then proceeds to criticize these positions.[19] Such a structure recalls the arguments of the tragedies. Dramatic tension accordingly enlivens the philosophical teaching. The next several sections of this chapter focus primarily on the connections between the themes of *Hercules Furens* and Senecan philosophical works such as the *Dialogues* and the *Moral Letters*. As observed above, the parody in *Apocolocyntosis* suggests that Seneca composed *Hercules Furens* some time before Nero's accession in 54 CE. During this period, Seneca served as a tutor to the youthful Nero.[20] O'Kell has accordingly suggested that one of the purposes of *Hercules Furens* was to serve as an education for the future emperor. Seneca's student would one day rule the Roman world, and so needed to be warned against "the potential to slip into tyranny and to destroy the world." As O'Kell observes, Hercules and the emperor both have "the power ... to exercise his will and to enact extremes of violence against the guilty and innocent alike. He is also a mortal struggling to come to terms with the potential bestowal of divinity . . . a Hercules who concludes the tragedy by rising to Theseus' challenge to regain his invincible spirit, to act with *magna . . . virtute* [great *virtus*], and to contain his anger could serve a didactic function as part of Seneca's educational programme for Nero."[21] The connection is intriguing, but like most biographical criticism it is ultimately unprovable, and many of Seneca's other tragedies contain warnings against tyranny.

Seneca's essay *On Mercy* is addressed directly to the emperor Nero, and *On Anger* contains numerous anecdotes about monarchs reviled due to their anger. In both essays, Seneca draws from tragedy to illustrate the point that a good ruler should be loved rather than feared by his people thanks to his gentleness and mercy toward them. He quotes from *Atreus* (no longer extant) by an earlier tragedian, Lucius Accius (*c.* 170–90s BCE), which had included a famous scene in which the tyrant proudly announced: "Let [the people] hate me, so long as they fear me" (Accius *Atreus* fr. 203–4). Seneca observes that the sentiment reflects the violent times of the dictator Sulla, who captured Rome in a civil war in 82 BCE and put many of his enemies to death (*On Anger* 1.20.4). As negative examples, Seneca tells numerous anecdotes of how the earlier emperors had used threats to force courtiers to perform cruel and embarrassing acts. A characteristic anecdote concerns the emperor Caligula (ruled 37–41 CE), who executed the son of Pastor, one of his courtiers, and then ordered Pastor to a dinner party with him on the same day. Seneca details how Pastor put on festive clothing, drank with the emperor, and did not once reveal his hatred of the man who had killed his son and now reclined next to him. "Why, you ask?" Seneca asks rhetorically in concluding the anecdote. "He had another son" (*On Anger* 2.33.5).

The tyrants of the tragedies similarly compel obedience through fear. In *Hercules Furens*, Lycus comments that "the first art of government / is putting up with hatred" (353–4) and then attempts to terrify Megara into marrying him. Seneca's own Atreus character, however, develops the theme of compelling the people through fear in a scene of *Thyestes* that likely recalls Accius's tragedy: "the best thing about being king / is making folks accept whatever you do / and even praise it" (*Thyestes* 205–7). Punishment in the afterlife traditionally awaits rulers such as these who abuse their power on earth. As he recalls his trip to the Underworld for Amphitryon, Theseus recalls how divine judges punished tyrants and urges others rulers like himself to be merciful: "O you who rule, / hold back from human blood! Your crimes are judged / more harshly than on earth" (745–7). These scenes from the tragedies were likely staged before members of the imperial court and reflect the ideas explored in the ethical essays. In both genres, Seneca instructs the emperor and members of the elite class in appropriate means of exercising monarchic power.

At the Crossroads: the allegorist's Hercules

Hercules had been an educational figure long before Seneca's time. In the fifth century BCE, the Greek philosopher Prodicus of Ceos told an influential parable of the "Choice of Hercules," in which the hero as a young man encounters the personifications of Virtue (*Aretē*) and Vice (*Kakia*) at a crossroads. (We conventionally translate *aretē* as "virtue," but, like Latin *virtus,* the word connotes "excellence" rather than the other-directed virtues that our culture values.) Each of these personifications attempts to persuade Hercules to choose her guidance for the future course of his life.[22] As Virtue explains in her speech that successfully persuades the hero to pursue excellence:

> I keep company with gods and good men, and no fair deed of god or man is done without my aid. I am first in honor among the gods and among men that are akin to me: to craftsmen a cherished fellow worker, to masters a faithful guardian of the house, to servants a kindly protector: a good helpmate in the toils of peace, a staunch ally

in the deeds of war, and the best partner in friendship . . . The young
rejoice to win the praise of the old; the elders are glad to be honored
by the young: with joy they recall their deeds past and are happy that
they are doing well in the present, for through me they are dear to
the gods, cherished by friends, precious to their native land.

Xenophon, *Memorabilia of Socrates* 2.1.32–3, tr. Marchant

In Prodicus's allegorized version, the Labors of Hercules represent a
pattern that all virtuous people can follow, whether or not they are
endowed with heroic strength and courage. Each person can fulfill
their obligations and win the respect of their fellow citizens. Prodicus'
Virtue is not blind to the hardships of the Labors, but assumes that all
right-thinking people would willingly seize the opportunity that they
provide to win eternal glory. Later writers adapted the parable of the
Crossroads and its personifications to narrate all kinds of choices
facing all kinds of heroes. In pre-Christian antiquity, these ranged
from the epic poet Silius Italicus' idealized account of how the youthful
Roman general Scipio began his career, to the satirist Lucian explaining
how he chose rhetorical Education (*Paideia*) over the Craft (*Technē*)
of sculpture when both personifications addressed him in a dream.[23]
Christian writers would quickly associate the Crossroads parable with
the moral choices faced by the followers of the new religion.[24]

Whether or not they appealed directly to the Crossroads allegory,
many ancient philosophers used Hercules' successful completion of
the Labors, culminating in his ascent to Olympus, as a model for
endurance through life's challenges. Cicero describes the "Herculean"
life of service to one's fellow human beings as an obligation for
everyone in accordance with human nature:

> In like manner it is more in accord with Nature to emulate the great
> Hercules and undergo the greatest toil and trouble for the sake of
> aiding or saving the world, if possible, than to live in seclusion, not
> only free from all care, but reveling in pleasures and abounding in
> wealth, while excelling others also in beauty and strength. Thus

Hercules denied himself and underwent toil and tribulation for the world, and, out of gratitude for his services, popular belief has given him a place in the council of the gods. The better and more noble, therefore, the character with which a man is endowed, the more does he prefer the life of service to the life of pleasure. Whence it follows that man, if he is obedient to Nature, cannot do harm to his fellow-man.

Cicero, *On Duties* 3.25, tr. Miller

Some of the views presented by the characters of Seneca's *Hercules Furens* resemble the arguments made by Vice and Virtue in Prodicus's fable. Virtue promises Hercules eternal fame if he undertakes the Labors. This outcome is precisely what Juno laments in her opening monologue: "the whole world / tells stories of his godhead" (39–40). Vice attempts to persuade Hercules to follow her in order to enjoy an easy and comfortable life. Seneca's Chorus similarly praise the quiet country life in the first ode, while Amphitryon laments at the beginning of Act 2 that the Labors have made his son suffer risks and hardship. Neither speaker, however, wants Hercules to become vicious as a result of having chosen an easier life. Amphitryon's concern is for his son's comfort and security, while the Chorus attribute moral failings to the ambitious rather than (as Prodicus did) to the lazy. In the latter half of Seneca's tragedy, these recollections of the terms of the Crossroads parable turn out to be misdirections. Hercules does return to the safety of his family in Thebes, enjoying his moment of triumph upon completing the Labors—but then engages in behavior far more vicious than Prodicus's Vice.

Prodicus's Hercules chooses a life of ambition and challenge over one of comfortable inactivity, but does not appear to have problems with madness. Other early allegorists, however, made him struggle against the vices of anger and desire rather than laziness and underachievement. A century after Prodicus, Herodorus of Heraclea on the Black Sea wrote an allegorized monograph on Hercules. In this version, Hercules' familiar attributes, the lionskin and club, and some of his trophies from the Labors, become symbols of human beings' struggle against anger and desire:

> They write that he wore a lion's skin instead of a tunic, carried a club, and got hold of three apples. These are the apples the myth says he took away after killing the serpent with his club, that is to say, after overcoming the worthless and difficult argument inspired by his keen desire, using the club of philosophy while wearing noble purpose wrapped around him like a lion's skin. Thus he took possession of the three apples, i.e., three virtues: to not grow angry, to not love money, and to not love pleasure. Through the club of his enduring spirit and the skin of his very bold and prudent argument he prevailed in his earthly struggle with petty desire, philosophizing until he died, as Herodorus, that very wise author, writes.
>
> Herodorus, *On Heracles* fr. 14, tr. Trzaskoma et al.

In Herodorus's allegory, as in *Hercules Furens*, Hercules has new monsters to face that come not from the far corners of the earth but from within himself. The allegorist transforms the warrior's weapons and trophies into the symbolic elements of a moderately ascetic practice of self-cultivation. The hero best known to the Greeks for his life of excess becomes a thoroughly unexpected model of self-control. Philosophy, "noble purpose," and lack of desire now guide his life rather than violence, glory, food, and sex. Though Seneca's philosophical letters and essays also offer similar guidance toward a life of self-cultivation,[25] his tragedy uses the figure of Hercules for a contrasting purpose. The tragic hero is not an Everyman facing everyday temptations like the figure discussed by the allegorists. Ordinary human beings are not invited to make Hercules' choices because we are not endowed with his divine strength. The first Chorus lays out the choice that we can make, between the retiring country life or the ambitious city life—not between staying at home or conquering the Underworld. If we are prey to the same delusions as Herodorus's

Hercules before he overcame them, then we cannot overcome them in the single day of *Hercules Furens*. Seneca discusses philosophy as a lifelong practice, in which ordinary people will alternately experience episodes both of successful advancement and degenerate backsliding on their way to achieving the perfection of the wise person (*sapiens*).

Seneca's lengthy descriptions of the world that Hercules moves through participate in the ancient literary tradition of moralizing landscapes and draw on pre-existing emotional associations with the place being described. In many of his *Moral Letters*, Seneca comments on the purpose of studying traditional narrative. Solving the problems of identifying mythical places, in his view, is less important than understanding the narrative's allegorical meaning and the moral warning associated with those places:

> Do you raise the question, 'Through what regions did Ulysses stray?' instead of trying to prevent ourselves from going astray at all times? We have no leisure to hear lectures on the question whether he was sea-tossed between Italy and Sicily, or outside our known world (indeed, so long a wandering could not possibly have taken place within its narrow bounds); we ourselves encounter storms of the spirit, which toss us daily, and our depravity drives us into all the ills which troubled Ulysses.
>
> Seneca, *Moral Letters* 88.7, tr. Gummere

The wise person will know to read the wanderings of Ulysses, the most famous of the great mythological travelers, as an allegory of the individual's daily struggle toward self-cultivation rather than simply as fantasy entertainment or puzzles for scholars who specialize in trivial details. In the same way, he or she will understand the exotic destinations of Hercules' Labors as part of an allegorized account, where Iberia, Scythia, and the Underworld represent different moral battlegrounds for the philosophical spirit.

Hercules' rage

Seneca commences the three-book essay *On Anger* with a memorable portrait of how ordinary people appear when they are driven mad by their anger:

> As madmen exhibit specific symptoms—a bold and threatening expression, a knitted brow, a fierce set of the features, a quickened step, restless hands, a changed complexion, frequent, very forceful sighing—so do angry people show the same symptoms: their eyes blaze and flicker, their faces flush deeply as the blood surges up from the depths of the heart, their lips quiver and their teeth grind, their hair bristles and stands on end, their breathing is forced and ragged, their joints crack as they're wrenched, they groan and bellow, their speech is inarticulate and halting, they repeatedly clap their hands together and stamp the ground, their entire bodies are aroused as they "act out anger's massive menace" . . .
>
> Seneca, *On Anger* 1.1.3–4, tr. Kaster

Amphitryon also very briefly recounts the symptoms that Hercules manifests when in the grip of rage ("Son, why are you frowning and shaking your face to and fro?" 953). The ordinary angry person, however, suffers from a different condition than the mad Hercules. The Stoics understood emotions such as anger as the result of the mind's conscious assent to "preliminaries" to emotion.[26] Everyone is constantly surrounded by countless frustrations and provocations to anger, particularly among Seneca's peers, an elite class obsessed with status competition. Under ordinary circumstances, however, it is within our power to choose whether or not to react to these "preliminaries" and become angry (*On Anger* 2.2.6). The wise person (*sapiens*) who successfully leads the philosophical life described in Seneca's ethical writings chooses not to "assent" to these provocations and allow them to become anger that leads him or her to act inappropriately. As Konstan explains, "the passions must be amenable to reason, or else they are beyond our control ... In the case of emotions—not the initial preliminaries to emotions, but genuine human emotions—reason must be able to prevail." When Seneca discusses the anger that often follows from "the mere opinion of an injury" (*On Anger* 2.2.2), Konstan observes that "the opinion alone is not enough: we must assent to it, for if this were not the case, we would not be in a position to withhold our assent and hence would be at the mercy of our passions."[27]

In *On Anger*, then, Seneca emphasizes that anger is a choice made in the conscious mind. What Juno has done by summoning the Fury to inflict madness on Hercules (982–6) is to remove his ability to perceive the world accurately and give or withhold his "assent" to the hallucinated "preliminaries" to emotion that he sees. He sees his own children as Lycus's children (987–1009), his wife as his hated stepmother Juno (1010–20). To argue that he consciously "assents" to murdering them when mad would imply that he either (a) secretly hated his wife and children and was only looking for an excuse to do away with them, for which there is no evidence in the play; or (b) is characteristically so violent and unrestrained that murdering his innocent loved ones means no more to him than brushing away flies. Neither interpretation would allow him to feel guilt upon waking to realize what he has done. Anger may be a form of temporary madness, but Hercules' madness is of a different order. In the Latin script, this would be the difference between *ira* (anger) and *furor* (madness). As Trinacty perceptively observes, the outcome nevertheless "follows one of Seneca's insights about *furor* ... namely, that it always directed in some sense against the agent who wields it."[28] As Hercules is the first to observe, having committed violence while in the grip of madness does not absolve him from responsibility and guilt.

Expressions of anger are implicit comments on social status. In a hierarchical, slave-holding society like imperial Rome, a person who

can rage unrestrainedly with impunity is likely toward the top of the
social scale. Punishment was the likely consequence for inferiors
who displayed anger at their superiors. In *Moral Letter* 47, Seneca
recommends that masters treat slaves kindly and mercifully, recalling
as they do that their slaves are fellow human beings. The exhortation
to be lenient is necessary because slaves are their masters' property
and so have no ability to protect themselves from their anger. Most of
the moral failings that Seneca discusses in *On Anger* are attributed to
monarchs and their courtiers, the figures who necessarily regard
everyone else as an inferior. It might therefore be thought that
Hercules, as the greatest of the heroes, should come equipped with
the greatest rage. In *On Anger*, however, Seneca urges his elite readers
not to mistake effect for cause. His peers may act out their anger
before their inferiors, but they should not mistake their impunity for
greatness of spirit:

> For that's not greatness; it's a swelling, just as when bodies are
> stretched taut by an abundance of unhealthy fluid. The disease is
> not an example of growth, but of destructive excess. All whose
> minds, in delirium, cause them to think more than human thoughts
> believe that they radiate something lofty, sublime. But there's no
> solid underpinning; rather, what has been raised up without a
> foundation is apt to come crashing down. Anger has no solid
> footing: it doesn't arise from something stable and destined to
> abide but is windy and empty, as far removed from greatness of
> spirit as recklessness is from bravery, arrogance from confidence,
> moroseness from sternness, cruelty from strictness.
>
> Seneca, *On Anger* 1.20.1–2, tr. Kaster

Though as observed above, Seneca's Hercules does not "assent" to his
anger, he nevertheless performs this familiar narrative of delirium
followed by collapse. The true "greatness of soul" that the ancients
ascribed to the allegorized Hercules derived from his ethical perfection
rather than his outsized rage.

The challenge of ambition

In the century before Seneca, the Roman poet Lucretius (*c.* 90s–50s BCE) used Hercules' Labors as a contrast to the philosopher Epicurus's more significant struggle against the vices and the passions. In the poet's view, the philosopher deserved the same admission into heaven that Hercules achieved, as his exploits were greater benefits to mankind than the hero's task of killing monsters. Human beings can choose to avoid the places where monsters dwell, but cannot escape assault by vice and passion and so must struggle every day against them:

> But if you think the deeds of Hercules rival his [Epicurus's], you will stray much farther still from true reasoning. For what harm could we now receive from that gaping maw of the Nemean lion, or from the bristling Arcadian boar? . . . And all the other monsters of this kind that were slain, if they had not been vanquished, what harm, pray, could they do alive? None, as I think, seeing how the earth even now teems with swarms of wild beasts, how full it is of unnerving terror through forests and great mountains and deep woods, which places it is mostly in our power to avoid. But unless the mind is purged, what battles and perils must then find their way into us against our will! How sharp then are the cares with which lust rends the troubled man, how great also the fears! Or what of pride, of filthy lust, of petulance? How great the devastation they deal! What of luxury and sloth? He [Epicurus] therefore who has vanquished all these and cast them forth from the mind by words, not by swords, will it not be proper that he be held worthy to be counted in the number of the gods?
>
> Lucretius, *On the Nature of Things* 5.22–51, tr. Rouse

Seneca the Stoic writes in a rival philosophical tradition from Lucretius the Epicurean. Yet the earlier poet's work is nonetheless a significant model for the Roman tradition of combining philosophy with poetry, and of using Hercules' Labors as the basic standard for praising a greater accomplishment. His example of a near-contemporary who deserves praise above Hercules is the younger Cato, the loyalist who opposed Caesar in the civil war (see above, p. 25). Like Lucretius's Epicurus, this wise man fought not wild beasts but the ambition that consumed the politicians of his era:

> For I said that the wise person can receive neither injury nor insult, and that the immortal gods had given Cato to us as a more reliable exemplar of the wise man than they had given Ulysses or Hercules to previous ages. Our fellow Stoics, you see, declared that these men were wise, being unbeaten by labors and being scorners of pleasure and victors over every kind of fear. Cato did not go into hand-to-hand combat with beasts, which are typically pursued by hunters and country dwellers, nor did he chase monsters with fire and steel, nor did he happen to live in times when it could be believed that the heavens rested on the shoulders of a single man ... He stood alone against the vices of a decadent city sinking under its own weight, and he kept a hold on the falling republic as much as it could be dragged back by just one hand.
>
> Seneca, *On the Constancy of the Wise Person* 2.1–2, tr. Ker

Given Hercules' traditional importance as a symbol of monarchic power, it is notable how poorly he administers power in Seneca's *Hercules Furens.* Lycus's taunting points to an inescapable truth: "is that slave more powerful than my throne?" (410). The "savior" has not been able to keep his own family on the throne of Thebes, while the "averter of evil" serves Eurystheus as a slave. Lycus's failure to understand that Hercules' heroism consists in endurance is widespread. In a later work, Seneca criticizes Alexander the Great for his misunderstanding in using the hero as a model. Alexander incorrectly assumed that Hercules was a robber rather than a peacemaker:

> ... slave as he [Alexander] was to glory, of which he knew neither the true nature nor the limitations, following the footsteps of Hercules and of Bacchus, and not even halting his course where they ceased, he turned his eyes from the givers of the honour to his

partner in it, just as if heaven, to which in supreme vanity he aspired, were now his because he was put on a level with Hercules! Yet what resemblance to him had that mad youth who instead of virtue showed fortunate rashness? Hercules conquered nothing for himself; he traversed the world, not in coveting, but in deciding what to conquer, a foe of the wicked, a defender of the good, a peacemaker on land and sea. But this other [Alexander] was from his boyhood a robber and a plunderer of nations.

Seneca, On Benefits 1.13.2–3, tr. Basore

Criticism of the long-dead Alexander permits Seneca to covertly criticize the powerful of his own day. He joins Hercules and Bacchus as comparisons to Alexander specifically to recall Virgil's praise of Augustus (*Aeneid* 6.801–5)—the first of the five emperors under whom Seneca lived. In a later section of the same essay, Seneca generalizes Alexander's vicious ambition to all lucky people who misuse their luck: "nor was this the vice of Alexander alone, whose successful audacity led him to follow in the footsteps of Bacchus and Hercules, but of all those whom Fortune has goaded on by rich gifts" (*On Benefits* 7.1.3, tr. Basore). For Seneca, then, to be a Hercules means not a search for material plunder but fighting an inner battle.

The challenges of Fortune

Most readers of these pages have likely not lived through war, famine, plague, or exile. The ancient world, however, was a far less stable and prosperous place than any part of the developed world today. The Greeks and Romans had little notion of how to calculate risks accurately and virtually no economic instruments to insure against them until late in the Renaissance.[29] Hercules' career accordingly provided an allegorical model of facing the prospect of adversity without anxiety and enduring unexpected calamities. Seneca catalogs examples of misfortune in one of the late *Moral Letters* to his friend Lucilius and explains how the wise person deals with them. Lucilius is aggrieved because his slaves have run away while he was on business. Seneca chides him for his frustration over what he regards as an unimportant matter, as any misfortune he can mention (robbery, blackmail, murder, flood, fire, etc.) has happened to others. The wise person accordingly recognizes life as a constant struggle and conforms to it rather than complaining that it has not treated him or her more easily. In the wise person's cheerful acceptance of whatever fate hands him or her, Seneca concludes, we find the true "greatness of soul" characteristic of the allegorized Hercules: "Here is your great soul— the man who has given himself over to Fate; on the other hand, that man is a weakling and a degenerate who struggles and maligns the order of the universe and would rather reform the gods than reform himself" (*Moral Letters* 107.12, tr. Gummere). Earlier in the letter, Seneca quotes two lines from Virgil's description of the personifications of Grief, Care, Sickness, and Old Age (*Aeneid* 6.274–5). In Seneca's letter, these personifications are no longer confined to residence in the Underworld but live with us constantly. Trinacty draws an association between this letter and *Hercules Furens,* where the hero's tragedy illustrates the challenges we all face on a grander scale:

> these personified "evils" are the very stuff of life, but now taken to a Herculean extreme. Characters such as Amphitryon and Hercules can persevere through the disease and grief that cause anguish in one's life. Through their reliance on friends and family, they can be given a helpful guide in one's old age or at least help one another endure the crucible of tragic suffering.
>
> Trinacty, *Senecan Tragedy*, p. 37

Like enemies in many of Seneca's tragedies, both Juno and Hercules call upon one another to watch a spectacle they have created. Juno threatens to show Hercules "hell on earth" (91), and Hercules orders

all the other gods to turn away from the polluting sight of Cerberus
and leave only Juno to watch his triumph (603–4). The created
spectacle is essential to the revenger's plot in the paradigmatic revenge
tragedies. Atreus's only regret as he completes his revenge in *Thyestes*
is that he cannot compel the gods to watch his triumph over his
brother (*Thyestes* 893–5), while Medea claims that she needs Jason to
be the "spectator" of her murder of the children (*Medea* 992–3). After
Juno's revenge on Hercules is complete, however, we are left with a
different kind of spectacle, the victim's struggle with his misfortune,
that the revenge plays curtail. According to Seneca, the gods admire
the sight of good men struggling with their adversity:

> I, for one, am not surprised if sometimes the gods have an impulse to
> watch great men wrestling with some calamity. Sometimes we feel
> pleasure if a young man with a steadfast mind has intercepted an
> oncoming beast with his hunting spear or has endured a lion's attack
> without showing any fear. This spectacle pleases us all the more in
> proportion to how nobly he accomplished it. [Yet] such childish and
> frivolous entertainments for human beings are not sufficient to attract
> the gods' attention. Here is a spectacle worthy to be looked on by god
> as he inspects his own creation; here is a god-worthy duel: a brave
> man matched against misfortune, especially if the man has issued the
> challenge himself.
>
> Seneca, *On Providence* 2.7–9, tr. Ker

The gods watch humans struggle with the challenges of their lives as if
watching a spectacle, just as Romans eagerly watched the beast-hunt
(*venatio*) that often formed the morning program at the arena games.
These are the rational gods of the providential Stoic universe, not the
angry Juno whose only interest is revenge. The "great man" is similarly
closer to the allegorized Hercules than to the monster-slayer of Seneca's
drama. Yet passages such as these could provide Seneca's audience with
an allegory of *Hercules Furens* Act 5 as well. Hercules' suffering dramatizes

the Stoic allegory of life as a spectacle engineered by a capricious Fortune, in which wise people prove their endurance under the eyes of the gods.

For Seneca, triumphing over real life's adversities is a greater challenge than Hercules' Labors, and the allegorical descriptions in the *Dialogues* make the wise person often appear more powerful than a Hercules. Seneca claims near the beginning of his essay *On the Constancy of the Wise Person* "that the wise person is vulnerable to no injury." No matter how many assaults wise people endure, none can affect their spirit:

> Just as the hardness of certain stones cannot be penetrated by iron, and adamant cannot be cut or crushed or worn away but actually blunts the things that hit it; just as certain things cannot be consumed by fire, but, even when surrounded by flames, still preserve their sturdiness and their form; and just as certain rocks projecting upward break the sea and yet show no traces of its ferocity despite being assaulted through the ages—just so solid is the wise person's mind, and it has gained such robustness that it is as safe from injury as those things I have recounted.
>
> Seneca, *On the Constancy of the Wise Person* 3.5, tr. Ker

The person who seeks to become wise, like the Lucilius of the *Moral Letters* who is slowly progressing along the endless path toward perfect wisdom, will in fact regard such challenges as opportunities to test his or her philosophical skills. In a letter instructing Lucilius not to fall prey to groundless anxieties, Seneca urges him to look back to his prior successes in overcoming Fortune's insults. Lucilius has successfully emerged from these contests like an experienced boxer whose earlier fights have made him more aware of his physical capacities (*Moral Letters* 13.2–3).

The allegory of Hercules' Labors as human beings' struggle against a variety of challenges (not all of which are physical) is comparable to Seneca's relentless use of combat metaphors in the *Dialogues* and *Moral Letters*.[30] Hercules' strength offers the concrete, visible physical analogue to the wise person's more abstract endowments, moral impregnability and firmness against anxiety. In Seneca's narrative of the philosophical life, the person who has achieved perfect self-cultivation is an experienced veteran of Fortune's battles, a gladiator who can never retire nor ask for pity, who must "die erect and unyielding" (*Moral Letters* 37.2). Just as the allegorized Hercules triumphed in every battle against monsters, wise people have triumphed in their spirits over all of Fortune's assaults, no matter how viciously Fortune has harmed their bodies, families, or property. To see Hercules consumed by despair and ready to commit suicide at the end of *Hercules Furens*, then, confirms that the wise person, no matter how physically unimpressive, is in fact far stronger than he.

Performance and Reception

Scholars of Roman tragedy reconstruct performance circumstances in the early imperial period from a paucity of evidence, and so must continue to question how and where Seneca's plays were performed. We have almost no evidence for the music, dance, and stage action that accompanied the performance. No ancient playscript includes stage or set directions; these must instead be inferred from the dialogue, and remain matters of scholarly debate. In addition, the medieval manuscripts that preserve the texts were copied long after Seneca's death. They sometimes present textual errors and varying attributions of dialogue to the characters. It is accordingly the editor's job to resolve such contradictions in the surviving textual evidence.[1]

The stage set for *Hercules Furens* consists at minimum of an altar, where Megara takes refuge from the tyrant Lycus, and a pair of doors behind center stage. These doors may either lead into the palace, as in most Senecan dramas, or possibly to a temple.[2] One wing of the stage is imagined to lead to the city, the other represents the path that Hercules and his companion Theseus take on their return from the Underworld. Evidence for the physical spaces in which Seneca's dramas were performed in his lifetime is sparse and contradictory. As discussed in previous chapters, lengthy descriptions (*ecphrases*) of landscape form a major component of the characters' speeches in *Hercules Furens,* culminating in Theseus' 100–line description of the Underworld. The extent and detail of these ecphrases have led some scholars to suggest that they take the place of a sophisticated theatrical set. On this view, the actor would sketch in the scene with words, and so enable the plays to be performed in a variety of spaces including private houses and recitation halls. Such a reconstruction works well for plays such as *Trojan Women*, where the characters describe different features of the ruined city of Troy and its surroundings.

In *Hercules Furens*, however, the majority of the descriptions concern places far from the palace at Thebes, the site of the play's action. These include the countryside praised in the opening chorus, the wild and distant places where Hercules performed his Labors, and the imaginary site of the Underworld. The point of most of these descriptions is to draw on the power of the audience's imagination through the use of evocative language and gesture. This was probably the case for the Trojan plays as well. Though it can complement the set designer's craft, Seneca's verbal art has independent goals. Marshall has argued that the plays may have been performed in aristocratic households, in a small three-sided indoor space or enclosed garden. The lengthy descriptions of the physical setting of each scene, in his view, suggest "a substitute for a physical set, rather than a complement to one."[3] Other scholars have argued for full-scale performance in large theaters.[4]

In Seneca's time, as in other periods of Greek and Roman theater, male actors wearing masks performed all of the roles in the tragedy. The masks and costuming indicated the identity of the mythological characters to the audience even before the actors began to speak. Masks reflected age, sex, and status: Amphitryon would have been easily recognizable from an old man's mask, Megara from a woman's white mask. Costuming likely helped to identify other characters, such as Hercules' lionskin and weapons, Lycus's royal dress, and so forth. The script of *Hercules Furens* does not specify the age and status of the Chorus, who are likely elderly male citizens of Thebes. Their masks would have made the details of their identity clear to the audience.[5] There is no indication of the number of Chorus members, and so scholars accordingly have proposed varying hypotheses. Calder suggested that Seneca's Choruses typically comprised between three and seven members, but as the Chorus speak as a group rather than with differentiated voices, Slaney has recently proposed the notion of a "Chorus of one."[6]

Actors playing the gods in tragedy typically appeared on the *mechane*, a crane that elevated them above the level of the human characters, and so the assumption has been that Juno does as well at the beginning of the play. This ancient theatrical convention gave rise to the expression *deus ex machina*, "the god from the machine." It refers to a god's sudden appearance at the end of the drama to resolve outstanding plot complications neatly, if not naturalistically. Seneca's Juno claims, however, that she has been evicted from Olympus by her husband's concubines, and so must live on earth because they occupy the sky (4–5). It has accordingly been suggested that the actor who plays the goddess may stand on the same stage level as the human characters, in order to represent Juno's residence on earth.[7] Like her threat to stand beside Hercules, however, Juno's words are likely figurative exaggerations, rather than a specific indication of her location on the stage. Juno leaves the stage at the end of her monologue and does not return for the remainder of the play. If she or the Fury stand beside Hercules, they do so only in the audience's imagination.

References to an altar and a temple in the dialogue of Act 2 have led scholars to speculate what structures may have occupied the stage. Lycus describes Megara's position on stage as follows: "she is here, by the altar's protection" (356). After their argument, he angrily tells her to "embrace the altars" (503), but immediately reveals that her hope of divine protection is futile. He orders his henchmen to pile up wood and set it on fire, so that the temple where Megara and the children are taking refuge will collapse on them (506–8). While an altar is a typical structure in many Greco-Roman tragedies, should we also imagine that this temple was also visible on stage? Some scholars propose that the doors at center stage should be envisioned as leading not to the palace, their typical direction in Greco-Roman tragedy, but to a shrine where Megara and

the children retreat after Lycus issues his command. Thus Hercules
would look at these doors when he arrives on stage and questions "but
why are foreign soldiers camped out by the temple, / besieging in full
arms the holy seat?" (616–17).[8] Other scholars more plausibly observe,
however, that these lines do not require reassigning the identity of the
building that lies behind the central doors, as the altar itself is sufficient
to suggest the presence of the temple that stood behind it.[9]

When Hercules and Theseus appear in Act 3, both men appear to
create a minor dramaturgical problem by addressing Megara (638–40).
Keeping Megara onstage is not a problem for modern directors, who
can cast as many actors as they wish or can afford to hire. But the scene
appears to challenge the ancient dramaturgical convention that only
three speaking actors plus the Chorus are ever on stage at the same
time. In an ancient staging, Megara would leave the stage at the end of
Act 2 to take refuge in the temple with the children. The actor who
played Megara in Act 2 would change his mask and costume in order
to play Hercules in Act 3, a practice called "doubling" on the modern
stage.[10] Kohn suggests that Hercules is "hallucinating" the presence of
Megara, and that Theseus has difficulty seeing the upper world after so
much time in the Underworld.[11] There is no need, however, to diagnose
madness in Hercules this early in the tragedy, as it would undercut the
dramatic impact of his hallucination in the middle of Act 4. Theseus's
vision problems would simply be confusing for the audience. Therefore,
it is equally plausible that both characters address Megara *in absentia*,
imagining how she must feel under threat from Lycus, just as she
addresses her husband *in absentia* throughout Act 2.

The scene of Hercules' murder of his family presents a number of
choices for a contemporary director. Should Megara and the children be
onstage when Hercules kills them? If so, how should the violence be
presented? The ancient director, however, faced a more limited set of
choices. A convention of the ancient theater forbade the representation
of violence on stage, though several scenes in Seneca's plays appear to

push this convention to its limits. Rather than portraying the killing of Megara and the children before the audience, Seneca assigns Amphitryon a running commentary on Hercules' actions. Hercules either leaves the stage to kill his first son (990), or remains onstage and shoots offstage. He leaves the stage to enter the palace to kill his second son (1001–2). He then pursues Megara out of the palace (1008–9) and runs offstage with her (1018), and kills her and his third son offstage. Megara's voice is heard from offstage as Hercules kills her.[12] He then returns to the stage (1035) and subsequently collapses. The bodies of Megara and the children are then displayed on a platform called the *exostra* pushed from the backstage.[13] When Hercules collapses, attendants remove his weapons. These roles would be assigned to non-speaking actors, a convention used for supernumerary characters such as slaves, children, soldiers, and other minor figures in the Greek and Roman theater.

From recitation drama to pantomime: reconstructing Senecan performance

Scholars used to view Seneca's tragedies as recitation dramas, meant to be read privately or performed as staged readings. This view derived from the nineteenth-century German Romantic critics, and continued through the mid-twentieth century.[14] Most scholars now accept performance in Seneca's day as a likelihood. The recitation drama theory arose from: (a) the paucity of evidence for tragic performance in Seneca's day; and (b) the fact that much of *Hercules Furens*, like the other Senecan tragedies, is taken up with description of events that do not occur on the stage. Examples begin as early as Juno's catalog of Jupiter's rape victims and illegitimate children transformed into stars (6–18) and continue with the narration of Hercules' Labors (215–48). It is difficult at first for many modern readers to understand the purpose of extremely lengthy speeches such as Theseus' description of the

Underworld (658–827), because they neither involve conflict nor advance the plot. In 1927, the American poet and critic T.S. Eliot (1888–1965) offered an influential diagnosis of what he saw as an aesthetic flaw in the play: "While Hercules is . . . engaged in a duel on the result of which everybody's life depends, the family sit down calmly and listen to a long description by Theseus of the Tartarean regions."[15] Eliot's verdict was representative of a nineteenth-century tradition unsympathetic to Seneca's rhetorical showpieces.

Ancient teachers of literature called this kind of lengthy description *ecphrasis.* Learning to describe all kinds of subjects in vivid language— living people, historical and mythological figures, cities and landscapes, works of art—was a basic part of the education of the young aristocratic Roman boys who grew up to attend performances of Senecan tragedy.[16] The Elder Seneca's collection of declamations preserves excerpts from declaimers of the Augustan era, who developed ecphrasis into high art and discussed its organic connections with modes of description in epic poetry. Ecphrastic speeches appear in every Senecan tragedy, as well as in other prestigious literary forms such as epic, and even in lighter genres such as love poetry and satire. A vast number of speeches of this type survive from antiquity, because ancient audiences greatly appreciated them. Rather than view Theseus' speech as digressive or fatal to dramatic suspense, Roman audiences would have appreciated aspects such as its development of Hercules' character; the beauty of its poetry (see in particular 698–706); its vision of justice in the afterlife; and its response to descriptions of the Underworld in the earlier epic tradition of Homer, Virgil, and Ovid. Eliot's criticism of Theseus' lengthy description of the Underworld, however, reflects nineteenth-century views of Senecan rhetoric and in turn proved formative for modern readers and audiences. Theater directors often severely truncate lengthy speeches such as this, while popular translations apologize for Seneca's rhetoric and learning, exactly the qualities that made him popular in antiquity and the Renaissance. Seneca's decisions make perfect sense for the audience that he addressed. Educated Romans knew the texts of the *Aeneid* and the *Metamorphoses* intimately and would have eagerly appreciated both the playwright's consummate display of his rhetorical skills and his sophisticated manipulation of the Augustan poetic tradition on the Neronian tragic stage.

More recently, scholars have examined the possible influence of pantomime on Senecan tragedy. These spectacles featuring celebrity dancers were very popular in the high Roman empire, and may have specialized in the violent scenes that tragedy generally kept offstage.[17] Lucian includes the madness of Hercules in his catalog of pantomime subjects (*On the Dance* 41). The late ancient scholar Macrobius attests to performance in the Augustan era of pantomimes featuring Hercules' madness. The actor Pylades of Cilicia, one of the founders of the genre of tragic pantomime, apparently disapproved of the audience's reaction to his performance as mad Hercules:

> When he had come on to dance *The Madness of Hercules*, some of the spectators thought that he was not keeping to action suited to the stage. Whereupon he took off his mask and rebuked those laughing at him with the words: "Fools, my dancing is intended to represent a madman." It was in this play too that he shot arrows at the spectators.
>
> Macrobius, *Saturnalia* 2.7.16–17, tr. Kaster

Impersonating Hercules, likely in the mode made popular by the pantomime, was also a favorite pastime of the emperors of Seneca's day. The historian Dio Cassius reports that the emperor Caligula:

> ... impersonated Hercules, Bacchus, Apollo, and all the other divinities, not merely males but also females, often taking the role of Juno, Diana, or Venus. Indeed, to match the change of name he would assume all the rest of the attributes that belonged to the various gods, so that he might seem really to resemble them. Now he would be seen as a woman, holding a wine-bowl and thyrsus, and again he would appear as a man equipped with a club and lion's skin or perhaps a helmet and shield.... Thus by varying the style of

his dress, and by the use of accessories and wigs, he achieved accuracy in many diverse parts; and he was eager to appear to be anything rather than a human being and an emperor.

Dio Cassius, Roman History 59.26.5–7, tr. Cary

Suetonius reports that Nero was interested in performing roles from tragedy, including the madness of Hercules:

> He also put on the mask and sang tragedies representing gods and heroes and even heroines and goddesses, having the masks fashioned in the likeness of his own features or those of the women of whom he chanced to be enamoured. Among other themes he sang *Canace in Labor, Orestes the Matricide, The Blinding of Oedipus* and *The Frenzy of Hercules.* At the last named performance they say that a young recruit, seeing the emperor in mean attire and bound with chains, as the subject required, rushed forward to lend him aid.

Suetonius, Nero 21.3, tr. Rolfe

Senecan tragedy features multiple "climactic moments" that occur at the conclusions of many of the acts as well as in the play's finale.[18] Zanobi has recently associated this aspect with pantomime, and argued that *Hercules Furens* Act 4 (895–1053) in particular "betokens the influence of pantomime."[19] In this scene, Amphitryon breathlessly narrates his son's killing of his family as it happens, rather than reporting it after the fact as the Euripidean messenger does. Yet instead of addressing his son directly, he describes his deeds in the third person. As Zanobi explains, he thereby adopts a convention of the pantomime, where an external narrator "remained aloof from the action" while describing the events enacted by the pantomime dancer.[20]

"Ercles' vein": Hercules in the Renaissance

Senecan tragedy in general, and the figures of the mad Hercules and the vicious tyrant in particular, were enormously influential on the

Renaissance stage. Hercules' madness provided Renaissance dramatists with "a rich and resident grammar of furor, an essential and expressive code of thought and feeling."[21] The Renaissance knew epilepsy as "Hercules' disease," *Herculanus* or *Herculeus morbus,* a tradition derived from the pseudo-Aristotelian *Problems.* In his collection of *Adages,* the Dutch polymath Desiderius Erasmus (1466–1536) explained that "it afflicted Hercules, either thanks to his immense Labors, or because Juno sent it upon him … The disease seems to be called *Herculean,* because just as Hercules was unconquerable, so it cannot be cured by any doctor's help."[22] The maddened hero's "raging madness followed by a palliative sleep" was so common in Renaissance tragedy that one scholar justly called it the "*Hercules Furens* convention."[23] I begin with a brief discussion of Seneca's influence on Shakespeare's contemporary Christopher Marlowe (1564–1593). The main part of the section focuses on William Shakespeare (1564–1616), whose adaptations of Seneca appear in his best-known plays.[24]

Marlowe's best-known play, *Tamburlaine the Great* (1587), draws its inspiration from the career of the Turko-Mongol warlord Timur (d. 1405). Hercules offered an attractive model for representing the conqueror who founded the Timurid dynasty, devastated much of western Asia, and led defeated kings in triumph. Slaney discusses the tragedy's adaptation of Senecan "excess" as it portrays "a Herculean hero operating at the limits of human capacity."[25] Conflict between the hero and the gods (theomachy) is a major thematic point of contact between the historical tragedy and its mythological ancestor. Seneca's Juno fears that Hercules will overthrow Jupiter and reign as king of heaven, and he indeed briefly threatens to do this during his episode of madness (955–73). Tamburlaine does not need to be driven mad to express theomachic ambitions, nor to attack his own family members. Even as his concubine Zenocrate pleads with him to make peace with her father, for example, Tamburlaine replies with a threat to overthrow the king of the gods: "Were *Egypt Joves* owne land, / Yet would I with my sword make *Jove* to stoope" (1 *Tamburlaine* 4.4.79–80). Tamburlaine later kills his son Calyphas, simply because the boy seems to be a coward unworthy to inherit his legacy as a conqueror. He again associates murder with theomachy: "For earth and all this airy region / Cannot contain the state of Tamburlaine" (2 *Tamburlaine* 4.1.119–20). As Chaudhuri observes: "whereas madness fully brought out Hercules' theomachic instincts, for Tamburlaine theomachy is rather the condition of his existence, the defining feature of his imperialist desires."[26] The first of Marlowe's plays to be performed on the London stage, it created immediate fame for its author, then only in his early twenties. Before this moment, classical theme and structure had largely featured in plays performed in English grammar-school classrooms, as part of students' classical education. *Tamburlaine* was one of the first English plays to take this dramatic idiom into the popular theatre, where it flourished throughout the succeeding century.

A survey of moments from four Shakespeare plays will suggest the range and intricacy of his negotiations with Seneca. As Hercules falls into a stupor after murdering his family, the Chorus pray for him to remain mad so he will not recognize his guilt (1094–9). In Shakespeare's *King Lear*, Gloucester makes the comparable wish to be mad like his King so he will not be aware of the calamities afflicting himself and his country: "Better I were distract: / So should my thoughts be sever'd from my griefs, / And woes by wrong imaginations lose / The knowledge of themselves" (*Lear* 4.6.281–4). Hercules wakes from his stupor at the beginning of Act 5, unaware of where he is and what he has done during his madness. He gradually realizes the significance of the blood on his hands and his devastated surroundings. Once fully aware of his responsibility for the murders, he suffers the overwhelming sense of guilt that initially leads him to seek escape in suicide. Shakespeare adapts this scene for one of *King Lear*'s emotional pinnacles, the scene in which the formerly mad king awakes from his stupor. Lear does not recognize his hands, his surroundings, nor his daughter Cordelia, whom he mistakes for one already dead:

> *Lear*: You do me wrong to take me out o' th' grave:
>   Thou art a soul in bliss, but I am bound
>   Upon a wheel of fire, that mine own tears
>   Do scald like molten lead.
> *Cordelia*: Sir, do you know me?
> *Lear*: You are a spirit, I know. Where did you die? . . .
>   Where have I been? Where am I? Fair daylight?
>   I am mightily abused. I should ev'n die with pity,
>   To see another thus. I know not what to say.
>   I will not swear these are my hands . . .
>   Methinks I should know you, and know this man;
>   Yet I am doubtful, for I am mainly ignorant
>   What place this is . . .
>   Do not laugh at me,
>   For as I am a man, I think this lady
>   To be my child, Cordelia.
>
> Shakespeare, *King Lear* 4.7.38–63

Hercules' realization of guilt begins his suffering, and his dead family members are in no position to forgive him. Lear has only banished his daughter Cordelia, however, not killed her, and so it is within her power to reunite with him and forgive him. Though father and daughter will not survive the play, their enemies' malice cannot remove that moment of reconciliation from them. Braden has written perceptively on Shakespeare's adaptation of the Senecan scene of Hercules' waking in order to enact "an experience of grace and forgiveness beyond anything that Seneca's fundamentally malevolent cosmos has to offer."[27]

At the end of Act 5, Amphitryon eventually persuades Hercules to choose exile over suicide. The hero's response characteristically shows that he views the world on a far larger scale than the human characters around him. Hercules recites a catalog of distant rivers at the edges of the Roman empire to impress upon his listeners that his guilt cannot be washed away:

> What Tanais or Nile or turbulent Tigris
> in Persia, or what wild barbarian Rhine
> or Tagus, flowing full with Spanish gold,
> could ever wash my hand? If icy Maeotis
> poured its frozen waters over me,
> and all the ocean ran across my hands,
> still my guilt sticks deep.
>
> Seneca, Hercules Furens 1322–9

Shakespeare's *Macbeth* repeatedly presents the motif that no water can wash away the guilt of murder. Immediately after killing King Duncan in order to seize the throne of Scotland, Macbeth stares in horror at his bloody hands and similarly denies that they can be washed clean:

> What hands are here? Ha, they pluck out mine eyes.
> Will all great Neptune's ocean wash this blood
> Clean from my hand? No, this my hand will rather
> The multitudinous seas incarnadine,
> Making the green one red.
>
> Shakespeare, Macbeth 2.2.57–61

Recollection of the Senecan Hercules' guilt emphasizes the viciousness of Macbeth's crime. Temporary insanity may exculpate Hercules, but Macbeth has killed with malice aforethought. Duncan was entitled to Macbeth's protection as his guest and to his loyalty as his king. The closeness of murderer and victim again recalls Hercules' violence. The combined motifs of madness and washing away guilt return most insistently at the beginning of Act 5, as Lady Macbeth expresses guilt in the form of compulsive handwashing: "Here's the smell of the blood still: all the perfumes of Arabia will not sweeten this little hand" (*Macbeth* 5.1.48–9).[28] Shakespeare's adaptation of the motifs from *Hercules Furens* Act 5 points to a different moral universe than

Seneca's, where evil cannot be blamed on a malevolent Juno but on human vices.

The hesitant Hamlet might seem an unlikely companion to the decisive Macbeth, and he feigns madness rather than raging like Lear or Othello. Yet like Hercules, Hamlet returns from abroad to face the usurper Claudius, who has made his tyranny acceptable to his people by marrying Hamlet's mother Gertrude, as Lycus had tried to marry Megara. Hamlet's early remark that his murderous uncle is his "father's brother, but no more like my father / than I to Hercules" (*Hamlet* 1.2.152–3) establishes the desirability for him of the standard set by Seneca's hero, who avenged the offenses to his family as quickly as others could describe them. Hamlet, by contrast, cannot decide whether the passion that he must summon for action is desirable. As Miola observes, "at times, Hamlet strives to enact the great passions of the Senecan avenger; at others he subscribes to the Stoic idea that passion is an infirmity, an emotional perturbation, ephemeral, savage, extreme, cruel, rude, not to trust."[29] The terms in which Hamlet works through this dilemma are Senecan. Shakespeare's greatest character contrasts the passionate action of the Senecan tragedies with the distanced reflection of the philosophical essays.

Seneca's tyrant Lycus also provided Renaissance drama with a model of the usurper who pursues power at the expense of justice, though this character was ultimately less influential than Atreus, the tyrant of Seneca's *Thyestes*. Lycus's courtship of Megara was a particular favorite for dramatists, in part because of the bravado required of the usurper and would-be lover.[30] Shakespeare adapted the scene early in *Richard III* to characterize his tyrant Richard, who has killed King Henry the Sixth and his son Edward, husband of Lady Anne. An early scene opens with Anne mourning beside Henry's corpse as it is carried through the streets. She rages: "Cursed be the hand that made these fatal holes! / Cursed be the heart that had the heart to do it!" (*Richard III* 1.2.14–15). Miola observes the parallels between the courtships of

Megara and Anne: "the similar preparations for entrance, the first
appeals on general principles, the tyrants' wish for a softer reply after a
bitter one, the justification for past slaughters, the violent reactions of
the women, both clad in garments of mourning, their wish for the
tyrant's death."[31] Yet the crucial difference is the outcome: though Anne
spits on Richard and curses him to hell, she ends up accepting him.
Lycus aims to reinvent himself as the legitimate monarch of Thebes
and to conceal the violence of his rise to power through marriage to
Megara. Richard similarly masquerades in a series of roles scripted for
him by others' expectations, including "the Concerned Brother, Smitten
Lover, Simple Fellow, Sage Counsellor, Reluctant Public Servant, Good
Uncle, Anointed King."[32] Both characters' efforts suggest the crude
reality of tyrannical power. They hold on to power through the threat
of force, will themselves into existence through speeches of self-
creation, and attempt to legitimize their rule by managing others'
perceptions.

Medieval and Renaissance readers loved to read quotable phrases, or
sententiae, from Seneca's tragedies. They collected them in *florilegia*,
anthologies of quotations from the classics.[33] The historical shift
in usage of the English word "sententious" shows why this aspect
of Seneca's writing was attractive to the Renaissance but became
problematic for the modern audience. Meaning 1 of the *Oxford English
Dictionary* entry for this word reads "full of meaning; also, of persons,
full of intelligence and wisdom." Illustrative quotations for this meaning
cover the period 1440–1646, which coincides with the period of Seneca's
greatest influence on the European stage. One way to think about the
power of the *sententia* is to recall a famous scene from Shakespeare's
Hamlet, Polonius' blessing of Laertes upon his son's departure from the
Danish court (*Hamlet*, Act 1, Scene 3). Modern actors often play
Polonius for laughs, as an irrelevant, senile fuddy-duddy, in keeping
with Hamlet's derisive comments about the man he will eventually kill.
Yet Shakespeare gave Polonius some of his most quotable lines in this

parting speech of advice: "the apparel oft proclaims the man," "neither a borrower nor a lender be," "to thine own self be true."[34] These phrases are *sententiae*: proverbial notions, pithily expressed. Meanings 3 and 4 of the *Oxford English Dictionary* entry show how the connotations of "sententious" have shifted in step with modern attitudes toward rhetoric: "in recent use sometimes in bad sense, affectedly or pompously formal," "of persons . . . now often in bad sense, addicted to pompous moralizing." Today's audiences do not like actors to preach at them, but audiences from antiquity through the Renaissance clearly did. Most classical scholars, however, now see Seneca's rhetoric as a virtue, and the *sententia* as a compressed form waiting to be rediscovered in the age of the tweet. As Braden observes, "the Renaissance ultimately does more justice to Seneca's subject matter and rhetoric than Seneca himself does."[35]

"The drama is all in the word": the modern reception of Seneca's rhetoric

Though Renaissance audiences responded eagerly to Seneca's virtuosic use of language, the critical reception of Seneca was severe from the eighteenth through the mid-twentieth centuries. It is only very recently that classical scholars have once more begun to appreciate the Senecan tragedies for what they are: powerful works of drama and poetry that have exerted enormous influence on Western theater. The verdict pronounced by the German Romantic critic August Wilhelm Schlegel (1767–1845) was decisive for the majority of nineteenth- and twentieth-century scholarly views. In Schlegel's memorable and endlessly quoted formulation, Seneca's tragedies were:

> beyond description bombastical and frigid, unnatural in character and action, revolting from their violation of every propriety, and so destitute of everything like theatrical effect, that I am inclined to believe they were never destined to leave the rhetorical schools for

the stage ... Their characters are neither ideal nor actual beings, but gigantic puppets, who are at one time put in motion by the string of an unnatural heroism, and at another by that of a passion equally unnatural, which no guilt nor enormity can appal.

Schlegel, *Course of Lectures*, pp. 162–3

Schlegel and his critical heirs could not deny the tremendous importance of Seneca's tragedies to the history of literature and theater. Yet they were content instead to dismiss the Renaissance's fascination with Seneca as an unfortunate aberration in the history of taste, caused by a forgivable veneration of all things ancient. Such hostile and limited views were canonized for scholarship by the influential German scholar Friedrich Leo (1851–1914), and inform T. S. Eliot's influential essay on Senecan tragedy. For Eliot, Seneca's "drama is all in the word, and the word has no further reality behind it. His characters all seem to speak in the same voice, and at the top of it; they recite in turn."[36]

Such views persisted almost until the present generation among classical scholars, and are still common in popular presentations of Senecan tragedy.[37] The recent turn in Seneca's critical fortunes depends on an assortment of factors. The Romantics created an enduring contrast in their stereotypes of classical Greek literature as "authentic," "natural," and "spontaneous," Roman literature as "decadent," "belated," and "artificial." Today, however, Schlegel and Eliot are no longer names for critics to conjure by. Contemporary scholars have emancipated themselves from the critical straitjackets of Romanticism, Modernism, and the New Criticism. They no longer see much value in locating dramas on a spectrum that runs from less to more "rhetorical" and "artificial". They pay close attention to the man behind the curtain instead of arguing that he should not call attention to himself. Certain types of discourse create the impression of authenticity and spontaneity better than others, and may be privileged in particular performance contexts. But that is all they are—effects demanded by particular audiences—rather than symptoms of a culture's "youth" or "decadence".

Modern performances of Seneca's *Hercules Furens* have been very few. It is also difficult for theater scholars to disentangle performances of the Senecan Hercules plays from those of scripts based on Euripides' *Heracles*. The *Archive of Performances of Greek and Roman Drama* (*APGRD*) lists eight performances of the play between 1549 and 2005.[38] Other performances drew on both the Euripidean and Senecan versions, such as *Hercole Perseguitato* (Lucca, 1657), *Megara Tebana* (Lisbon, 1788), *Héraklès* (Paris, 1953), and *Gerakl* (unidentified location in the Soviet Union, 1986).[39] The evidence for some of these performances is ambiguous, however, and others represent "distant relatives," in the terminology of the *APGRD*. The most authentic example of modern staging of Seneca's *Hercules Furens* is likely a Parisian production, *Hercule Furieux*, at the Théâtre Gérard Philipe de Saint-Denis, Paris, in 1996. Directed by Jean-Claude Fall from a translation by Florence Dupont, this staging occurred as the culmination of a series of revivals of Seneca's tragedies in two Parisian theatres in 1995–6.[40]

Combat Trauma and the Undoing of Hercules

In his *Mad Heracles*, Euripides presents the goddess Lussa intervening to drive Heracles mad, but also highlights other exogenous explanations for the hero's descent into madness. Euripides' Amphitryon asks his son: "My son, what has come over you? What is this change you have undergone? Surely it was not the blood of the men you just killed that has made you mad?" (Euripides *Heracles* 965–7, tr. Kovacs). The Greeks may not have had a word for it, as they did for so many other medical conditions. Yet the community of citizen-soldiers that attended the play may have recognized very well what Americans have at various times called "shell shock," "battle fatigue," "post-traumatic stress disorder," and now call combat trauma. Modern scholars have understood passages such as these which relate violence against family to past experience as part of a "missing diagnosis" of combat trauma in Athenian culture.[41] By contrast, the audience of Roman aristocrats that attended Seneca's tragedies likely had little first-hand experience of combat trauma. Some may have served in the officer corps but would have not likely seen hand-to-hand combat. Wars in the early Roman Empire were infrequent and fought in distant locations by an increasingly professionalized military under the direct control of the emperor. None of Seneca's audience found themselves in the battle for survival that the Peloponnesian War would become for Euripides' Athenian audience. If combat trauma may not have been relevant for Seneca's audience, it has been the major point of connection for modern audiences of both Hercules plays.

Combat trauma is still not a well understood medical condition, but some characteristics such as poor impulse control and sudden episodes of violence have been well documented in popular media. Hercules' unexpected outburst of violence against his family, followed by an equally abrupt collapse into a stupor, fits a pattern that modern readers are tempted to associate with the domestic violence perpetrated by veterans of the Iraq and Afghanistan conflicts.[42] Contemporary directors have been attracted to both the Greek and Latin Hercules dramas through their representation of symptoms that appear similar to combat trauma. Adaptations of Euripides' better-known version have led the way. Anne Carson's translation of Euripides' *Heracles* (2006) "defined Herakles' madness specifically as 'berserker furor.'"[43] In Simon Armitage's *Mister Heracles* (2000), commissioned by the West Yorkshire Playhouse in Leeds, UK, the character is a "living, breathing, one-man case-history" of psychiatric trauma.[44] As Riley observes, "Armitage is even more explicit than Seneca in internalizing the germ of violence."[45] More distant adaptations include the Canadian Opera Company's 2014 production of Handel's opera *Hercules*. Director Peter Sellars emphasized the connection between the Hercules myth and the modern American soldier's experience of combat trauma.[46]

This section focuses on one example of the mature tradition of representing Hercules as a victim of combat trauma: the 2013 production of *Hercules Furens (The Madness of Hercules)* by the Los Angeles-based Not Man Apart Physical Theatre Ensemble. John Farmanesh-Bocca, the director, views *Hercules Furens* as "one of the first plays written that addresses the existence of PTSD in soldiers after battle."[47] The play was first commissioned and performed in 2011 by the Getty Villa in Malibu, California (see Fig. 3).

A revised version was presented as a world premiere in 2013 at the Miles Memorial Playhouse in Santa Monica, California. Farmanesh-Bocca adapted, directed, and starred in the title role of the 65–minute production. The director added a series of allegorical characters, such as "Pleasure," "Virtue," "Wrath," and "Fury," to the Getty cast. The set consisted of a bare stage with a few rough-hewn sculptures recalling classical male nudes. The Santa Monica world premier featured additional roles for the god Apollo and two children, while two of the personifications, Pleasure and Virtue, remained as "Nymphs of Juno." In both productions, Farmanesh-Bocca cut Theseus' role in order "to streamline the play to the absolute essence."[48]

Physical theater was the primary means, in Farmanesh-Bocca's view, of "allow[ing] the audience to make their own connection to the modern day warriors." The actors' postures often referenced those of classical sculptures. A three-man Chorus (including Jones Welsh, the current director of the company) joined Farmanesh-Bocca's Hercules in enacting much of the action that Seneca leaves as description, including the Labors and the descent to the Underworld. This narrative strategy also enabled the company to present Hercules' murders of his family members as if through the maddened hero's own eyes rather than from the audience's objectively distanced perspective.[49] Farmanesh-Bocca slowly wrestled the members of the Chorus, delusively identifying them as he did so as the monsters of the Labors. (Contrast, for example, the decision made by Jean-Claude

Fig. 3 Not Man Apart Physical Theater Company, *Hercules Furens.*
John Farmanesh-Bocca, Deus Xavier, Andrew Heffernan, and Jones Welsh.

Fall to use stroboscopic light on a darkened stage to present Hercules' madness as he kills his family.[50]) After Farmanesh-Bocca's collapse into a stupor after committing the murders, the Chorus returned with the bodies of Hercules' wife Megara (Courtney Munch) and children and placed them in the same postures as the "monsters" that the hero thought he had killed. As Farmanesh-Bocca observed, his character:

> wakes up to the reality of what was happening [along] with the audience. That way you're [the audience member] completely on the perspective of the person with PTSD. You're completely on the tragedy of losing the family but you went with him on that journey, you saw how it came to pass. *Hercules* ended up being one of our most emotional pieces.

Farmanesh-Bocca's modernization of the characters' dialogue and affective responses also contributed to the play's emotional connection with audiences. The characters of the play mostly spoke in classicizing dialogue, except for Randolph Rand's Lycus, who spoke entirely in contemporary American vernacular. One reviewer likened his character to the American TV comedian Jon Stewart.[51] The usurper's vernacular emphasized his role as an outsider among the Thebans who does not share their values. Another reviewer observed that Apollo Dukakis's Amphitryon "witnesses Lycus's abuse of Megara and later tries to provide a path forward for the grieving Hercules; his perspective also provides a path for modern audiences to enter the story more fully."[52] The absence of a Theseus character in the fifth act meant that Amphitryon talked Hercules down from suicide without assistance. Reviews, however, tended to feature many of the characteristic complaints brought against Senecan drama in the modern era: "a strange blend of rhetoric, philosophy, psychology, and exaggeration."[53]

Farmanesh-Bocca grew up in a military family; his older brother is a military doctor and Iraq war veteran. Not Man Apart presented the play as part of a series of adaptations from Shakespeare and classical theater that focus on the experience of the warrior returning home from battle. These include *Titus Redux* (2010), an adaptation of Shakespeare's *Titus Andronicus* staged at the Kirk Douglas Theater in Los Angeles. Farmanesh-Bocca played Titus as "a traumatized American general back from fighting not the Goths but the Taliban," who experiences flashbacks of his combat experiences.[54] After the 2011 *Hercules Furens* production, Not Man Apart next produced *Lysistrata Unbound* (2013) at the Getty Villa Theater Lab, starring Olympia and Apollo Dukakis. Aristophanes' comedy fantasizes that the women of ancient Athens attempted to end the Peloponnesian war by refusing to sleep with their husbands. Playwright Eduardo Machado's "prequel" tells the story of how their leader Lysistrata became "the most celebrated peace activist of the ancient world."[55] The company's most recent production, *Ajax in Iraq* (2014), is Ellen McLaughlin's "mashup" of Sophocles' *Ajax* with interviews with war veterans. As Farmanesh-Bocca observed, the quartet presents "four different viewpoints of war: either from home observing the war [*Lysistrata*], *Hercules* taking in the aftermath of war, *Titus* delves into the madness very much the same way *Hercules* did." The goal of the quartet was to show "what [war] means to the warrior class, what the warrior class means to society, what war means to the elite class." In the current era of technologized and distant warfare, only a relatively small percentage of Americans know an active-duty soldier or a veteran suffering from combat trauma.[56] Farmanesh-Bocca continues to emphasize the importance of using classical theatre to bring veterans' experiences to the public.

"Zero to Hero": avoiding madness in contemporary comics and film

I conclude by discussing the tendency to veer away from representing Hercules' episode of madness in contemporary popular media. The film *Hercules* (dir. Pietro Francisci, 1958), starring Steve Reeves, inaugurated the American craze for "peplum" pictures upon its US release in 1959. This film initially presents Hercules as solo adventurer and lover. A young Ulysses tells him that "women are a nuisance. At first you suffer because you want a wife, then you suffer because you're jealous, and when your jealousy has passed you end up suffering because she bosses you around!" When Hercules encounters the princess Iole, however, he tells her that "I want to live like any other mortal man. It's my prayer to have a family. I want children of my own." He appears to gain his wish as they sail off into the sunset at the end of the film. The series of adventure films that followed pitted Hercules against increasing unlikely foes (including vampires, Incas, and "Moon Men"), but did not stray far from the formula that initially appealed to Joseph Levine, the film's American promoter: "musclemen, broads, and a shipwreck and a dragon for the kids."[57]

Almost forty years later, the Disney film *Hercules* (1997) included some of the familial aspects of the myth in a story aimed at children, but carefully "sanitized" them. Here Hera becomes Hercules' kindly biological mother and Alcmene and Amphitryon his loving foster parents. In place of the malevolent stepmother, Hades, the god of the underworld, seeks to destroy Hercules by sending the monsters of the Labors to destroy him, but Hercules' victories only serve to increase his fame. The film relates the youthful and naïve hero's romance with "Meg" (Megara), who begins as an ally of Hades who seeks to lure Hercules to destruction. She then evolves into Hercules' loving supporter as he demonstrates his "honesty and integrity." As Blanshard and Shahabudin observe, "when Hercules declares to Megara 'I will never hurt you', the viewer who knows their mythology is left to laugh at the ironic humor of the statement and the boldness of Disney's sanitization of the myth." Marriage between them initially seems an impossibility as Meg dies and Hades tricks Hercules into giving up his divine powers. Hercules rescues Meg, however, from death by offering to trade his life for hers. Thanks to his willingness to sacrifice himself, his divinity is restored, and he can attack Hades. After visiting his divine parents on Olympus, who confirm that he is now a "true hero," Hercules returns to Thebes to live happily ever after with Meg. The Disney version's retelling "represent[s] a desire to repress notions of domestic violence, irrational anger, and sexual transgression in favor of a world view that celebrates monogamous companionate relationships and the nuclear family."[58]

A grimmer version of Hercules, as acknowledged murderer of his family and victim of combat trauma, appears in Moore and Wijaya's graphic novel *Hercules: The Thracian Wars* (2008). Hercules and his followers serve the Thracian king Cotys as mercenaries to help him unite the local tribes under his domination. One of Cotys's arrogant courtiers wants to know if the hero really is the son of a god, or if his mother Alcmene has simply disguised mortal infidelity as divine rape. Another courtier sarcastically observes that Hercules "has these murderous rages, as well, where he'll just kill anyone, too. Even his own children, apparently. Blames that on the goddess Hera, who's 'persecuting' him!"[59] The skepticism regarding the hero's birth and deeds recalls *Hercules Furens* Act 2, in which Lycus questions the reality of the Hercules legend. In *Thracian Wars,* the narrator Iolaus murders the sneering Thracian courtier (calling him a "flabby bastard"), which merely encourages rather than rebutting this skepticism. Moore and Wijaya offer a more nuanced view of combat trauma than many contemporary popular Hercules narratives. This Hercules reflects one of the major issues in the reintegration of contemporary veterans into civilian society, the desire to return to the order, camaraderie, and psychological intensity of military life. Iolaus the narrator speculates that Hercules "came to Thrace to lose himself in the role of plain mercenary soldier." The hero suffers a brief episode of depression after his lover Meneus is killed by a sniper: "Being half-god himself, was it any wonder Hercules fell into titanic griefs?" Hercules is no berserker, however, and holds the soldiers back on numerous occasions from foolhardy assaults: "When you've fought all your life you grow weary. And cautious. 'Heroism' is a madness that strikes young men."[60] Moore assigns the role of berserking madman to Hercules' companion Tydeus, who continues to slaughter "like a rabid dog" when others have ceased from fighting. Tydeus also seeks to eat his unfortunate victims' brains, and his hideous appetites become a recurring motif in each chapter. Moore's Hercules is certainly a psychologically damaged hero, but not one who has become too dysfunctional to thrive in civilian society like Tydeus.

Brett Ratner's film *Hercules* (Paramount/MGM, 2014) excises the elements of *Hercules: The Thracian Wars* that challenge the image of the heteronormative family man familiar from the Disney cartoon. The film was loosely based on Moore and Wijaya's comic series. Shortly before his death, however, Moore attempted to disassociate himself from the production, for which he apparently received no compensation.[61] At the beginning of the film, Hercules (Dwayne Johnson) believes that he has killed his family and suffers from hallucinations in which he is visited by the three-headed dog Cerberus. Near the end, however, imprisoned by the Thracian king Cotys (John Hurt), he receives a visit from Eurystheus (Joseph Fiennes). Eurystheus reveals that he drugged Hercules and sent three wolves to kill Hercules' family. This unexpected adaptation of elements of Hercules' final Labor prompted both the hero's guilt and his hallucinations. Hercules gets to take ironically appropriate vengeance on his enemies by crushing them under a statue of his divine enemy Hera. Two subplots of Moore and Wijaya's novel focus on Hercules' sexuality: his pre-existing relationship with his lover Meneus, whose death in battle sends him into depression; and his brief affair with the princess Ergenia, king Cotys's daughter, who seduces him in order to find out his secrets and causes his imprisonment by betraying him to her father. Ratner's version removes both of these sexual relationships: Meneus is transformed into Hercules' cousin, and Hercules must rescue Ergenia (Rebecca Ferguson), along with her son Arius, from death at the hands of her scheming father. The mother and child become stand-ins for the family he has lost. In Ratner's modestly successful film, Hercules becomes an uncomplicated hero who desires heterosexual family love and whose goals are to learn how to "believe in himself" and to discover "the true nature of heroism." We are back in the familiar tradition of Joseph Levine's series of Hercules films and Disney's cartoon *Hercules.* The murderer of the hero's family is eventually revealed to be the villain, and the ending offers an uplifting moral message. We prefer to watch a simpler Hercules in the twenty-first century rather than contemplate Seneca's grim insight that the hero can be remade into his own worst enemy.

Notes

Preface

1 Recent biographies of Seneca include Romm, *Dying Every Day*; Wilson, *Greatest Empire*; Griffin, *Seneca*.
2 Slaney, *Senecan Aesthetic*, p. 3.

1: Introducing *Hercules Furens*

1 For the meter of Seneca's choruses, see Mazzoli, "Chorus".
2 Ovid, *Metamorphoses* 2.401–530. See Chapter 3 for discussion.
3 Examples include Virgil *Georgics* 2.458–540 and Horace *Satires* 2.6. The rhetoric teacher Quintilian, who taught at Rome in the generation after Seneca, discusses as a typical theme for student debate: "whether city or country life is better" (Quintilian, *The Orator's Education* 2.4.24).
4 For images of Hercules traveling to Olympus on a chariot, see Munich 2360, an Attic red figure pelike, *c.* 410 BCE. http://www.perseus.tufts.edu/hopper/artifact?name—unich+2360&object=Vase [accessed 1 September 2016]
  For the Roman triumph, see Beard, *Roman Triumph*.
5 See Schmidt, "Space and Time," pp. 541–2.
6 See Heil, "Vision, Sound."
7 See Mazzoli, "Chorus," pp. 567.
8 See Trinacty, *Senecan Tragedy*, pp. 146, 152.
9 Sutton, *Seneca on the Stage*, pp. 41–2, argues that Theseus' words mark the entry of a second Chorus. Kohn, *Dramaturgy*, p. 102, observes that reentry by the same Chorus is more likely; it avoids a crowded stage and confusion about the Chorus's identity.
10 See Mazzoli, "Chorus," p. 567.
11 See Fitch, *Seneca's Hercules Furens*, p. 335.
12 See Mazzoli, "Chorus," p. 567.

13 See Chapter 4 (p. 84ff.) and Fitch, *Seneca: Tragedies*, 1.17.
14 Wyles, "Heracles' Costume," p. 194.
15 See Schmidt, "Space and Time," p. 537.

2: Major Themes in *Hercules Furens*

1 See Hook, "Nothing Within."
2 See Bloomer, *School of Rome*, pp. 170–92.
3 See Heil, "Vision, Sound, and Silence"; Fitch, *Seneca: Tragedies*, p. 1.
4 See Griffiths, *Euripides: Heracles*.
5 See Fitch and McElduff, "Construction of the Self," p. 36.
6 See Harrison, "Themes," p. 623.
7 See Riley, *Reception and Performance*, pp. 64–5; Lawall, "*Virtus* and *Pietas*."
8 See Billerbeck, "*Hercules Furens*"; Mader, "Form and Meaning."
9 See Billerbeck, "*Hercules Furens*," p. 430.
10 See Fischer, "Systematic Connections," pp. 754–8.
11 *Oxford English Dictionary*, meaning 1a.
12 *Oxford Latin Dictionary*, meanings 1a–b.
13 Aristotle, *Nicomachean Ethics* 2.2.
14 See Fitch, *Seneca's Hercules Furens*, p. 163.
15 See Mader, "Form and Meaning," pp. 18–19.
16 See Sklenár, *Taste for Nothingness*.
17 See Leigh, "Lucan and the Libyan Tale."
18 See Edwards, *Death in Ancient Rome*, pp. 113–43.
19 See Reydams-Schils, *Roman Stoics*, pp. 45–52.
20 See Fischer, "Systematic Connections," p. 762.
21 For the propagandistic use of ancestors, see Baroin, "Remembering One's Ancestors." For the invention of legendary ancestors, see Wiseman, "Legendary Genealogies."
22 See Frank, "The Rhetorical Use of Family Terms"; Ginsberg, "Don't Stand So Close to Me."
23 Saller, *Patriarchy, Property*, p. 88.
24 See Littlewood, *Self-representation and Illusion*, p. 32.
25 Seneca *Moral Letters* 44.1–2, tr. Gummere.

26 Seneca *Moral Letters* 44.3–4.

27 See Bernstein, "Each Man's Father"; Gardner, *Family and Familia*, pp. 114–208.

28 See Goldberg, "Greek and Roman Elements," pp. 641–3.

29 The settings of Seneca's *Moral Letters* are similarly moralized: see Henderson, *Morals and Villas.*

30 See Shaw, "Eaters of Flesh".

31 For example, Pindar *Nemean Ode* 3.20–3. As Fitch observes (*Seneca's Hercules Furens*, p. 195), accounts of Hercules' creation of the Straits of Gibraltar only appear elsewhere in much later sources, such as Diodorus Siculus *Library of History* 4.18.5 (first century BCE) and Pliny *Natural History* 3.4 (first century CE).

32 For the representation of Hercules' encounters with Sleep and Old Age on Attic vases, see Stafford, "Vice or Virtue?", pp. 81–4.

33 Fitch's translation of *frendens Dolor* (*HF* 693) is more accurate in this respect than Wilson's "pain".

34 Trinacty, "Senecan Tragedy," p. 33.

3: Monster-slayer, Moral Exemplar, and Madman: Hercules' Ancient Roles

1 These include 3,520 images listed under "Herakles," and 416 under "Herakles/Hercle."

2 See Chaudhuri, *War with God*, pp. 116–55.

3 A representative example occurs in the appendix to Miller, *Seneca: Tragedies*, pp. 526–36, which presents "Comparative Analyses" of the plays on facing pages. For modern comparisons more sensitive to Seneca's goals, see Riley, *Reception and Performance*, Ch. 2; Braden, "Heracles and Hercules."

4 See Braden, "Heracles and Hercules."

5 See [Apollodorus] *Library of Greek Mythology* 2.4.12; Griffiths, *Euripides: Heracles*, pp. 20–1.

6 See Griffiths, *Euripides: Heracles*, p. 83.

7 Wyles, "Heracles' Costume," p. 195.

8 See Zeitlin, "Thebes."

9 See Provenza, "Madness and Bestialization."

10 See Galinsky, *Herakles Theme*, pp. 81–100.

11 It must be emphasized that the total number of such images is very small. The *Lexicon Iconographicum Mythologiae Classicae* lists only six entries from the total of nearly 4,000 images of Herakles ("Herakles" #1684–9). Some of the six entries are literary descriptions of lost works. Another example of an image depicting the scene comes from a Roman villa in Torre de Palma, Portugal (*c.* 300–400 CE) as shown on the cover.

12 Pache, *Baby and Child Heroes*, p. 57. See Taplin, *Pots & Plays*, #45.

13 Scholion to Pindar *Isthmian* 4.104g = *FGrH* 3 F 14. See Pache, *Baby and Child Heroes*, pp. 52, 57.

14 Wyles, "Heracles' costume," p. 188. Wyles describes Heracles' costume, as follows: he wears an "elaborate plumed helmet and greaves, a *chlamys* (short cloak) decorated with stars and a border, and a transparent fringed *exomis* (*chiton* fastened at one shoulder). Strings of pearls hang down over his *chiton* and a set binds his upper arm" (p. 188).

15 The passages from Plautus' *The Merchant* (*Mercator*) may be based on an earlier Greek play by Philemon entitled "The Merchant" (*Emporos*); see Wyles, "Heracles' Costume," p. 191 n34.

16 See Stewart, *Faces of Power*, p. 93.

17 For the lion skin worn by Alexander, see Athenaeus, *The Learned Banqueters*, 12.537f.; for his successors' adoption of the costume, see Rawlings, "Hannibal and Hercules."

18 See Feeney, *Gods in Epic*, pp. 155–62.

19 Putnam, "Virgil's Tragic Future," p. 257. See also Hardie, "Virgil and Tragedy."

20 For divine rape in Ovid, see Richlin, "Reading Ovid's Rapes."

21 Pentheus: Ovid *Metamorphoses* 3.511–733; Philomela: Ovid *Metamorphoses* 6.401–674.

22 Hinds, "Seneca's Ovidian *Loci*," p. 10; see Seneca *Oedipus* 709–12.

23 Hubris: Galinsky, *Heracles Theme*, pp. 168–70. "Moral Feebleness": Henry and Walker, "Futility of Action." Overreaching: Shelton, *Seneca's Hercules Furens*, p. 70. For the survey of negative opinions, see Motto and Clark, "*Hercules Furens: Maxima Virtus*," pp. 261–6.

24 Putnam, "Virgil's Tragic Future," p. 254.

25 See Trinacty, *Senecan Tragedy*, pp. 130–8.

26 See Trinacty, *Senecan Tragedy*, pp. 13–14.

4: *Hercules Furens* and Seneca's career

1 See Roncali, "*Apocolocyntosis*"; Freudenburg, "Seneca's *Apocolocyntosis*."

2 See Tacitus, *Annales* 14.53–5 and Seneca *On the Happy Life* 17.2.

3 For this tradition, see Ker, *Deaths of Seneca*.

4 For the possibility of performance, see Freudenburg, "Seneca's *Apocolocyntosis*," p. 96.

5 Trinacty, *Senecan Tragedy*, pp. 6–7.

6 The other two extant Roman tragedies include a play relating Hercules' death, *Hercules on Oeta*, and an historical drama, *Octavia*. Some Renaissance readers incorrectly attributed these works to Seneca.

7 For a history of Roman tragedy, see Erasmo, *Roman Tragedy*.

8 See Quintilian *The Orator's Education* 8.3.31, 10.1.98; Tacitus *Annals* 11.13; and Tacitus *Dialogue on Oratory* 13.7. See also Goldberg, "Greek and Roman Elements," on the question: "what did 'tragedy' mean to Romans of Seneca's class in Seneca's generation?" (p. 646).

9 For the centrality of the theme of the "golden mean" in Senecan choruses, see Mader, "Form and Meaning".

10 Bartsch, "Senecan Selves," p. 188.

11 See Gill, "Seneca and Selfhood," p. 67.

12 Star, "Commanding *Constantia*," p. 208.

13 See Boyle, *Tragic Seneca*, pp. 15–31.

14 If you don't yet read Latin, but want to appreciate some of its expressive potential, see Fitzgerald, *How to read*.

15 For Seneca's moral teaching through maxims, see Chaumartin, "Philosophical Tragedy?" pp. 657–8.

16 See Braund, "Seneca *Multiplex*."

17 See Romana Berno, "Exploring Appearances."

18 Williams, *Cosmic Viewpoint*, p. 255. See Seneca, *Questions About Nature* 6.32.4.

19 See Roller, "Dialogue in Seneca's *Dialogues.*"

20 See Tacitus, *Annals* 12.8; Suetonius, *Nero* 7.1.

21 O'Kell, "*Hercules Furens* and Nero," pp. 192, 194, 197.

22 See Xenophon, *Memorabilia of Socrates* 2.1.21-34. For discussion, see Stafford, "Vice or Virtue?"

23 Silius Italicus *The Punic Wars* 15.18–128; Lucian *The Dream, or Lucian's Career* 6–16.

24 For the post-classical history of the Crossroads parable, see Galinsky, *Herakles Theme*, pp. 185–230.

25 For the elements of the Senecan practice of self-cultivation, see Bartsch, "Senecan Selves," pp. 189–90; Ker, "Seneca on Self-Examination."

26 For fuller discussion, see Graver, *Stoicism and Emotion.*

27 Konstan, "Senecan Emotions," pp. 177–8.

28 Trinacty, *Senecan Tragedy*, pp. 133–4. See *On Anger* 1.1, 1.5.2, 1.7.4, 2.35.5, 3.1.5, 3.28.1.

29 For a history of risk calculation and economic tools to minimize risk, see Bernstein, *Against the Gods.*

30 For an introduction to Seneca's characteristic metaphors, see Armisen-Marchetti, "Seneca's Images and Metaphors."

5: Performance and Reception

1 Recent editions of the Latin text include Fitch, *Seneca: Tragedies*, and Billerbeck, *Seneca:* Hercules Furens.

2 Fitch, *Seneca: Tragedies*, vol. 1, p. 47, describes the doors as leading to the palace.

3 See Marshall, "Location!", p. 33.

4 See Kohn, *Dramaturgy*, pp. 1–14.

5 See Sutton, *Seneca on the Stage*, pp. 35–6.

6 Three to seven members: Calder, "Size"; one singer, Slaney, "Seneca's Chorus".

7 See Kohn, *Dramaturgy*, p. 97.

8 See Kohn, *Dramaturgy*, pp. 95–6.

9 See Fitch, *Seneca: Tragedies*, vol. 1, p. 47, and Fitch, *Seneca's* Hercules Furens, p. 248.

10 Two different doubling schemes are possible: Lycus/Hercules, Juno/ Amphitryo, Megara/Theseus (Sutton, *Seneca on the Stage*, p. 29), or Juno/Lycus/Theseus, Megara/Hercules, Amphitryo (Kohn, *Dramaturgy*, p. 4).

11 See Kohn, *Dramaturgy*, p. 94.

12 See Fitch's notes to these lines and Zanobi, *Seneca's Tragedies*, pp. 104–5.

13 See Kohn, *Dramaturgy*, p. 104.

14 See Heil, "Vision, Sound, and Silence"; Kohn, *Dramaturgy*, pp. 1–14; Fitch, "Playing Seneca?"

15 Eliot, *Selected Essays*, 69.

16 On declamation in Roman education, see Bloomer, *School of Rome*, pp. 170–92; on ecphrasis, see Webb, *Ekphrasis*.

17 Zanobi, *Seneca's Tragedies*, pp. 13–14.

18 See Zanobi, *Seneca's Tragedies*, pp. 70–1.

19 See Zanobi, *Seneca's Tragedies*, pp. 103–5.

20 Zanobi, *Seneca's Tragedies*, p. 105.

21 See Miola, *Shakespeare*, p. 122. In general, see Braund, "Haunted by Horror."

22 Erasmus *Adagia* 2.4.27 (#1327). See Soellner, "Madness of Hercules"; Riley, *Reception and Performance*, p. 99; Miola, *Shakespeare*, p. 131.

23 See Miola, *Shakespeare*, p. 123; Soellner, "Madness of Hercules."

24 See Boyle, *Tragic Seneca*, pp. 141–66.

25 Slaney, *Senecan Aesthetic*, p. 83.

26 Chaudhuri, *War with God*, p. 325. See also Boyle, *Tragic Seneca*, pp. 169–70.

27 See Braden, "Herakles and Hercules," p. 260.

28 For the theme of hands in *Macbeth*, see Miola, *Shakespeare*, pp. 112–17.

29 Miola, *Shakespeare*, p. 55.

30 See Miola, *Shakespeare*, p. 82.

31 Miola, *Shakespeare*, p. 83.

32 Miola, *Shakespeare*, p. 76.

33 See Fitch, *Seneca's Hercules Furens*, pp. 59–61.

34 As any educated Renaissance man would, Polonius also knows his Seneca. He instructs the Players who perform at the Danish court: "Seneca cannot be too heavy, nor Plautus too light" (*Hamlet*, Act 2, Scene 2).

35 See Braden, "Herakles and Hercules," p. 257.

36 Eliot, *Essays*, p. 7.

37 For example, Watling's Penguin translation (*Four Tragedies*, 1966) was for a long time the main modern English translation widely available to the general reader. Watling cannot imagine the possibility of full-dress performance and can barely imagine recitation.

38 http://www.apgrd.ox.ac.uk/productions/canonical-plays/hercules-furens/360 [accessed 1 September 2016]. The first performance listed (Nuremberg, 1549) is attributed to an Italian traveling company which may have presented either Seneca's *Hercules Furens* or Plautus' *Amphitruo* (http://www.apgrd.ox.ac.uk/productions/production/8052) [accessed 1 September 2016].

39 *Hercules Furens* (Oxford, 2005) was also performed in English translation in the chapel of Brasenose College, Oxford, 9–13 May 2005. *APGRD* lists no information regarding director, cast, or reviews.

40 See http://www.apgrd.ox.ac.uk/productions/production/3707 [accessed 1 September 2016]; Davis, *Seneca: Thyestes*, pp. 35–6; Mayrhofer, "Complete Plays".

41 See Konstan, "Combat Trauma". As Rabinowitz, "Women and War," observes: "The play shows very clearly and explicitly the interrelated nature of warfare, trauma leading to madness, and war on the family" (p. 196).

42 For readings of ancient texts informed by psychiatric work with military veterans, see Shay, *Achilles in Vietnam* and *Odysseus in America*.

43 Riley, *Reception and Performance*, p. 310.

44 Armitage, *Mister Heracles*, p. 51. For discussion, see Riley, *Reception and Performance*, pp. 312–37; Griffiths, *Euripides: Heracles*, p. 26.

45 Riley, *Reception and Performance*, p. 313.

46 See Wachtel, "Peter Sellars."

47 Not Man Apart Physical Theater Ensemble, "Hercules Furens."

48 All citations of Farmanesh-Bocca not otherwise attributed are from an interview with author, 5/15/2015.

49 Barrett, "Not Man Apart," described this production as "suitable to ages 10 and above."

50 As Mayrhofer, "Complete Plays," observes, "When normal light was restored, the tableau of the corpses was mirrored in a life-size model fixed high up on the back wall of the stage, already transported to the sky, as it were."

51 Frankel, "*Hercules Furens.*"

52 Shirley, "Adapting *Saturday Night Fever*, Shakespeare and Seneca."

53 Frankel, "*Hercules Furens.*"

54 Boehm, "Shakespeare's 'Titus Andronicus'".

55 Getty Museum, "Villa Theater Lab."

56 Fallows, "Tragedy of the American Military," observes that "at the end of World War II, nearly 10 percent of the entire US population was on active military duty." In contrast, the percentage of the American population on active military duty is much lower in the present generation: "a total of about 2.5 million Americans, roughly three-quarters of 1 percent, served in Iraq or Afghanistan at any point in the post-9/11 years, many of them more than once."

57 See Blanshard and Shahabudin, *Classics on Screen*, p. 63.

58 Blanshard and Shahabudin, *Classics on Screen*, pp. 203, 212–13.

59 Moore and Wijaya, *Hercules: The Thracian Wars*, issue 1, p. 6.

60 Moore and Wijaya, *Hercules: The Thracian Wars*, issue 3.

61 Shannon, "Alan Moore Calls for Boycott."

Further Reading

Senecan studies have enjoyed a revival of interest in the decade since Davis and Mayer contributed their volumes to the *CGRT* series. Though including the classic works of scholarship, this annotated guide focuses primarily on the more recent scholarly and popular additions to the bibliography.

Life and works of Seneca

Asmis, Elizabeth, Shadi Bartsch, and Martha C. Nussbaum, eds. 2010. *The Complete Works of Lucius Annaeus Seneca*. Chicago, IL: University of Chicago Press.
New translations of Seneca's philosophical works.

Bartsch, Shadi, and Alessandro Schiesaro. 2015. *The Cambridge Companion to Seneca*. Cambridge: Cambridge University Press.
A collection of essays on various aspects of Seneca's life, writings, and reception.

Damschen, Gregor, and Andreas Heil, eds. 2014. *Brill's Companion to Seneca: Philosopher and Dramatist*. Leiden: Brill.
A comprehensive volume featuring chapters introducing each of Seneca's philosophical and dramatic works.

Fitch, John G. 2008. *Seneca: Oxford Readings in Classical Studies*. Oxford: Oxford University Press.
A collection of important scholarly articles on Seneca's philosophical writings and tragedies.

Griffin, Miriam T. 1992. *Seneca: A Philosopher in Politics*. Oxford: Oxford University Press.
A comprehensive biography of Seneca and his relationships with the various emperors under whom he wrote.

Griffin, Miriam T. 2013. *Seneca on Society: A Guide to De Beneficiis*. Oxford: Oxford University Press.
An introduction to the philosophical, sociological, and historical significance of Seneca's treatise *On Benefits*.

Ker, James. 2009. *The Deaths of Seneca*. Oxford: Oxford University Press.
A study of major themes in Seneca's writings and the reception of his work in the Renaissance and modern period.

Romm, James. 2014. *Dying Every Day: Seneca at the Court of Nero*. New York: Alfred A. Knopf.
A biography that focuses primarily on the later years of Seneca's life, his interactions with members of the imperial court, and the writings he produced during this period.

Wilson, Emily. 2014. *The Greatest Empire: A Life of Seneca*. Oxford: Oxford University Press.
A biography of Seneca that contextualizes his writings.

Seneca and Roman tragedy

Boyle, A.J. 1997. *Tragic Seneca: an essay in the theatrical tradition*. London: Routledge.
An introduction to Seneca's tragedies and their impact on Renaissance and modern drama.

Boyle, A.J. 2006. *An introduction to Roman Tragedy*. London: Routledge.
A study that places Seneca in the context of the genre of Roman tragedy.

Erasmo, Mario. 2004. *Roman Tragedy: Theatre to Theatricality*. Austin, TX: University of Texas Press.
A history of the development of Roman tragedy and its interactions with Roman culture.

Fitzgerald, William. 2013. *How to Read a Latin Poem: If You Can't Read Latin Yet*. Oxford: Oxford University Press.

Aimed at the reader who does not yet know the Latin language, this book introduces some aspects of Latin's expressive potential and some of the basic conventions of Latin poetry.

Harrison, George W.M. 2000. *Seneca in Performance*. London: Duckworth.
Reviews the evidence for ancient performance of Seneca's tragedies and examines selected modern productions of Seneca.

Kohn, Thomas D. 2013. *The Dramaturgy of Senecan Tragedy*. Ann Arbor, MI: University of Michigan Press.
A systematic study of dramaturgical issues in each of the eight tragedies attributed to Seneca.

Slaney, Helen. 2016. *The Senecan Aesthetic: A Performance History*. Oxford: Oxford University Press.
A comprehensive study of Seneca's influence on subsequent Western theatre.

Translations, adaptations, and performances

Archive of Performances of Greek and Roman Drama. http://www.apgrd. ox.ac.uk/ [accessed 30th August 2016].
A comprehensive database of materials relating to "the performance of ancient texts in any medium and any period, from Greek tragedy to Roman epic, from stage to screen, from antiquity to the present day."

Bolt, Ranjit. 1999. *Seneca: Hercules (The Madness of Hercules)*. London: Oberon Books.
A lyric translation that presents dialogue as rhyming couplets and choruses as quatrains.

Fitch, John G. 2002. *Seneca: Tragedies*. 2 volumes. Cambridge, MA: Harvard University Press.
Presents the text of all of Seneca's tragedies in Latin with facing English translations.

Slavitt, David R. 1992. *Seneca*. Baltimore, MD: Johns Hopkins University Press.
An unreliable, idiosyncratic translation.

Watling, E.F. 1966. *Seneca: Four Tragedies and Octavia*. Harmondsworth: Penguin.
For a long time the only popular translation widely available in English, but superseded by more recent translations such as Wilson's.

Wilson, Emily. 2010. *Seneca: Six tragedies*. Oxford: Oxford University Press.
The best available translation of Seneca's *Hercules Furens*.

Studies of the Hercules tradition

Blanshard, Alastair. 2005. *Hercules: A Heroic Life*. London: Granta.
A composite narrative of the life of Hercules and his reception.

Galinsky, G. Karl. 1972. *The Herakles Theme: The Adaptations of the Hero in Literature from Homer to the Twentieth Century*. Oxford: Blackwell.
Surveys the hero's impact on Western culture.

Griffiths, Emma. 2006. *Euripides: Heracles*. London: Duckworth.
A survey of the key themes of Euripides' play.

Riley, Kathleen. 2008. *The Reception and Performance of Euripides' Herakles: Reasoning Madness*. Oxford: Oxford University Press.
A comprehensive survey of the reception of both the Euripidean and Senecan versions of the play in literature and performance.

Stafford, Emma. 2012. *Herakles*. New York: Routledge.
A survey of Hercules' various roles in Greco-Roman antiquity.

Bibliography

Archive of Performances of Greek and Roman Drama. http://www.apgrd.ox. ac.uk/ [accessed 30 August 2016]

Armisen-Marchetti, Mirelle. 2015. "Seneca's Images and Metaphors." In Bartsch and Schiesaro, 150–60.

Asmis, Elizabeth, Shadi Bartsch, and Martha C. Nussbaum, eds. 2010. *The Complete Works of Lucius Annaeus Seneca*. Chicago, IL: University of Chicago Press.

Baroin, Catherine. 2010. "Remembering One's Ancestors, Following in Their Footsteps, Being Like Them: The Role and Forms of Family Memory in the Building of Identity." In V. Dasen and T. Späth, eds. *Children, Memory, and Family Identity in Roman Culture*. Oxford: Oxford University Press, 19–48.

Barrett, Shari. 6/7/2013. "Not Man Apart Physical Theater Presents Thrilling Staging of *Hercules Furens*." http://www.broadwayworld.com/los-angeles/ article/BWW-Reviews-Not-Man-Apart-Physical-Theater-Presents-Thrilling-Staging-of-HERCULES-FURENS-20130607 [accessed 30 August 2016]

Bartsch, Shadi. 2015. "Senecan Selves." In Bartsch and Schiesaro, 187–98.

Bartsch, Shadi, and Alessandro Schiesaro. 2015. *The Cambridge Companion to Seneca*. Cambridge: Cambridge University Press.

Bartsch, Shadi, and David Wray, eds. 2009. *Seneca and the Self*. Cambridge: Cambridge University Press.

Beard, Mary. 2007. *The Roman Triumph*. Cambridge, MA: Harvard University Press.

Bernstein, Neil W. 2008. "Each Man's Father Served as His Teacher: Constructing Relatedness in Pliny's *Letters*." *Classical Antiquity* 27(2): 203–30.

Bernstein, Peter L. 1996. *Against the Gods: The Remarkable Story of Risk*. New York: John Wiley & Sons.

Billerbeck, Margarethe. 1999. *Seneca: Hercules Furens*. Leiden: Brill.

Billerbeck, Margarethe. 2014. "*Hercules Furens*." In Damschen and Heil, 425–33.

Billerbeck, Margarethe, and Sophie Guex. 2002. *Sénèque, Hercule Furieux.* Bern: P. Lang.

Bishop, J. David. 1966. "Seneca's *Hercules Furens*: Tragedy from *Modus Vitae.*" *Classica et Mediaevalia* 27: 216–24.

Blanshard, Alastair. 2005. *Hercules: A Heroic Life.* London: Granta.

Bloomer, W. Martin. 2011. *The School of Rome: Latin Studies and the Origins of Liberal Education.* Berkeley, CA: University of California Press.

Boehm, Mike. 8/29/2010. "Shakespeare's 'Titus Andronicus' returns to battle." http://articles.latimes.com/2010/aug/29/entertainment/la-ca-0829-titus-redux-20100829 [accessed 30 August 2016].

Bolt, Ranjit. 1999. *Seneca: Hercules (The Madness of Hercules).* London: Oberon Books.

Boyle, A.J. 1997. *Tragic Seneca: An Essay in the Theatrical Tradition.* London: Routledge.

Boyle, A.J., ed. 1983. *Seneca Tragicus: Ramus Essays on Senecan Drama.* Berwick, VIC: Aureal Publications.

Boyle, A.J. 2006. *An Introduction to Roman Tragedy.* London: Routledge.

Braden, Gordon. 1970. "The Rhetoric and Psychology of Power in the Dramas of Seneca." *Arion* 9: 5–41.

Braden, Gordon. 1984. "Senecan Tragedy and the Renaissance." *Illinois Classical Studies* 9: 277–92.

Braden, Gordon. 1985. *Renaissance Tragedy and the Senecan Tradition: Anger's Privilege.* New Haven, CT: Yale University Press.

Braden, Gordon. 1993. "Heracles and Hercules: Survival in Greek and Roman Tragedy (with a Coda on *King Lear*)." In Scodel, 245–64.

Braund, Susanna. 2013. "Haunted by Horror: The Ghost of Seneca in Renaissance Drama." In Emma Buckley and Martin T. Dinter, eds. *A Companion to the Neronian Age.* Malden, MA: Wiley-Blackwell, 425–43.

Braund, Susanna. 2015. "Seneca *Multiplex:* The Phases (and Phrases) of Seneca's Life and Works." In Bartsch and Schiesaro, 15–28.

Calder, William M. 1975. "The Size of the Chorus in Seneca's *Agamemnon.*" *Classical Philology* 70: 32–5.

Chaumartin, François-Régis. 2014. "Philosophical Tragedy?" In Damschen and Heil, 653–69.

Chaudhuri, Pramit. 2014. *The War with God: Theomachy in Roman Imperial Poetry*. Oxford: Oxford University Press.

Costa, C.D.N., ed. 1974. *Seneca*. London: Routledge.

Damschen, Gregor, and Andreas Heil, eds. 2014. *Brill's Companion to Seneca: Philosopher and Dramatist*. Leiden: Brill.

Davis, P.J. 2003. *Seneca: Thyestes*. London: Duckworth.

Edwards, Catharine. 2007. *Death in Ancient Rome*. New Haven, CT: Yale University Press.

Eliot, T.S. 1956. *Essays on Elizabethan Drama*. New York: Harcourt, Brace and Company.

Erasmo, Mario. 2004. *Roman Tragedy: Theatre to Theatricality*. Austin, TX: University of Texas Press.

Fallows, James. January/February 2015. "The Tragedy of the American Military." *The Atlantic*. http://www.theatlantic.com/features/archive/2014/12/the-tragedy-of-the-american-military/383516/ [accessed 30 August 2016].

Farmanesh-Bocca, John. 15 May 2015. Interview with author.

Feeney, D.C. 1991. *The Gods in Epic: Poets and Critics of the Classical Tradition*. Oxford: Oxford University Press.

Fischer, Susanna E. 2014. "Systematic Connections between Seneca's Philosophical Works and Tragedies." In Damschen and Heil, 745–68.

Fitch, John G. 1987. *Seneca's Hercules Furens: A Critical Text with Introduction and Commentary*. Ithaca, NY: Cornell University Press.

Fitch, John G. 2002. *Seneca: Tragedies*. 2 volumes. Cambridge, MA: Harvard University Press.

Fitch, John G. 2008. *Seneca: Oxford Readings in Classical Studies*. Oxford: Oxford University Press.

Fitch, J.G., and S. McElduff. 2002. "Construction of the Self in Senecan Drama." *Mnemosyne* 55: 18–40.

Fitzgerald, William. 2013. *How to Read a Latin Poem: If You Can't Read Latin Yet*. Oxford: Oxford University Press.

Frank, Marica. 1995. "The Rhetorical Use of Family Terms in Seneca's *Oedipus* and *Phoenissae*." *Phoenix* 49: 121–30.

Frankel, Tony. 11 June 2013. "*Hercules Furens* (The Madness of Hercules): Not Man Apart at Miles Memorial Playhouse in Santa

Monica." http://www.stageandcinema.com/2013/06/11/hercules-furens-not-man-apart/ [accessed 30 August 2016].

Freudenburg, Kirk. 2015. "Seneca's *Apocolocyntosis*: Censors in the Afterworld." In Bartsch and Schiesaro, 93–105.

Fuller, David, and Edward J. Esche, eds. 1998. *The Complete Works of Christopher Marlowe*. Oxford: Clarendon Press.

Galinsky, G. Karl. 1972. *The Herakles Theme: The Adaptations of the Hero in Literature from Homer to the Twentieth Century*. Oxford: Blackwell.

Gardner, Jane F. 1998. *Family and Familia in Roman Law and Life*. Oxford: Clarendon Press.

Getty Museum. "Villa Theater Lab." http://www.getty.edu/museum/programs/performances/theater_lab.html [accessed 30 August 2016].

Gill, Christopher. 2009. "Seneca and Selfhood: Integration and Disintegration." In Bartsch and Wray, 65–83.

Ginsberg, Lauren Donovan. 2015. "Don't Stand So Close to Me: Antigone's *Pietas* in Seneca's *Phoenissae*." *Transactions of the American Philological Association* 145: 199–230.

Goldberg, Sander M. 2014. "Greek and Roman Elements in Senecan Tragedy." In Damschen and Heil, 639–52.

Graver, Margaret. 2007. *Stoicism and Emotion*. Chicago, IL: University of Chicago Press.

Griffin, Miriam T. 1992. *Seneca: A Philosopher in Politics*. Oxford: Oxford University Press.

Griffin, Miriam T. 2013. *Seneca on Society: A Guide to* De Beneficiis. Oxford: Oxford University Press.

Griffiths, Emma. 2006. *Euripides: Heracles*. London: Duckworth.

Hardie, Philip R. 1993. *The Epic Successors of Virgil: A Study in the Dynamics of a Tradition*. Cambridge: Cambridge University Press.

Hardie, Philip R. 1997. "Virgil and Tragedy." In Charles Martindale, ed. *The Cambridge Companion to Virgil.* Cambridge: Cambridge University Press, 312–26.

Harrison, G.W.M. 2000. *Seneca in Performance*. London: Duckworth.

Harrison, G.W.M. 2014. "Themes." In Damschen and Heil, 615–38.

Heil, Andreas. 2014. "Vision, Sound, and Silence in the 'Drama of the Word.'" In Damschen and Heil, 547–60.

Henderson, John. 2004. *Morals and Villas in Seneca's Letters: Places to Dwell.* Cambridge: Cambridge University Press.

Henry, Denis, and B. Walker. 1965. "The Futility of Action: A Study of Seneca's *Hercules Furens.*" *Classical Philology* 60: 11–22.

Herington, C.J. 1966. "Senecan Tragedy." *Arion: A Journal of Humanities and the Classics* 5(4): 422–71.

Hill, D.E. 2000. "Seneca's Choruses." *Mnemosyne* 53: 561–87.

Hill, T.D. 2004. Ambitiosa Mors: *Suicide and the Self in Roman Thought and Literature.* London: Routledge.

Hinds, Stephen. 2011. "Seneca's Ovidian *Loci.*" *Studi Italiani di Filologia Classica* 9: 5–63.

Hook, Brian S. 2000. "'Nothing within which passeth show': Character and *Color* in Senecan Tragedy." In Harrison, 53–71.

Hunter, G.K. 1974. "Seneca and English Tragedy." In Costa, 166–204.

Kaster, Robert A. 2005. *Emotion, Restraint, and Community in Ancient Rome.* Oxford: Oxford University Press.

Kaster, Robert A., and Martha C. Nussbaum. 2010. *Seneca: Anger, Mercy, Revenge.* Chicago, IL: University of Chicago Press.

Ker, James. 2009. *The Deaths of Seneca.* Oxford: Oxford University Press.

Ker, James. 2009. "Seneca on Self-Examination: Rereading *On Anger* 3.36." In Bartsch and Wray, 160–87.

Kohn, Thomas D. 2013. *The Dramaturgy of Senecan Tragedy.* Ann Arbor, MI: University of Michigan Press.

Konstan, David. 2014. "Combat Trauma: The Missing Diagnosis in Ancient Greece?" In Meineck and Konstan, 1–14.

Konstan, David. 2015. "Seneca's Emotions." In Bartsch and Schiesaro, 174–84.

Lawall, Gilbert. 1983. "*Virtus* and *Pietas* in Seneca's *Hercules Furens.*" In Boyle 1983, 6–26.

Leigh, Matthew G.L. 2000. "Lucan and the Libyan Tale." *Journal of Roman Studies* 90: 95–109.

Littlewood, Cedric A.J. 2004. *Self-representation and Illusion in Senecan Tragedy.* Oxford: Oxford University Press.

Mader, Gottfried. 1990. "Form and Meaning in Seneca's 'Dawn Song' (*HF* 125–201)." *Acta Classica* 33: 1–32.

Mader, Gottfried. 2002. "Masks and the Man: Atreus, Lycus and Performances of Power in Seneca." In P. Defosse, ed. *Hommages à Carl Deroux I.* Bruxelles: Latomus, 336–47.

Marshall, C.W. 2000. "Location! Choral Absence and Dramatic Space in *Troades*." In Harrison, 27–51.

Mayrhofer, Colin. 1996. "The Complete Plays of Seneca. Theatre des Quartiers d'Ivry; Theatre Gerard Philipe de Saint-Denis, October 1995 to February 1996." *Didaskalia* 3(1): http://www.didaskalia.net/issues/vol3no1/mayrhofer.html [accessed 30 August 2016].

Mazzoli, Giancarlo. 2014. "The Chorus: Seneca as Lyric Poet." In Damschen and Heil, 561–74.

Meineck, Peter, and David Konstan, eds. 2014. *Combat Trauma and the Ancient Greeks.* New York: Palgrave MacMillan.

Miles, Geoffrey. 1996. *Shakespeare and the Constant Romans.* Oxford: Clarendon Press.

Miller, Frank Justus. 1917. *Seneca: Tragedies.* London: William Heinemann.

Miller, Walter. 1913. *Cicero. On Duties.* Cambridge, MA: Harvard University Press.

Miola, Robert S. 1992. *Shakespeare and Classical Tragedy: The Influence of Seneca.* Oxford: Oxford University Press.

Moore, Steve, and Admira Wijaya. 2008. *Hercules: The Thracian Wars.* Carpenteria, CA: Radical Publishing.

Motto, Anna L., and John R. Clark. 1981. "*Maxima Virtus* in Seneca's *Hercules Furens*." *Classical Philology* 76: 101–17.

Motto, Anna L., and John R. Clark. 1988. *Senecan Tragedy.* Amsterdam: A.M. Hakkert.

Motto, Anna L., and John R. Clark. 1993. *Essays on Seneca.* Frankfurt am Main: P. Lang.

Motto, Anna L., and John R. Clark. 1994. "The Monster in Seneca's *Hercules Furens* 926–39." *Classical Philology* 89: 269–72.

Nees, Lawrence. 1991. *A Tainted Mantle: Hercules and the Classical Tradition at the Carolingian Court.* Philadelphia, PA: University of Pennsylvania Press.

Nicgorski, Ann M. 2005. "The Magic Knot of Herakles and the Propaganda of Alexander the Great." In Rawlings and Bowden, 97–128.

Not Man Apart Physical Theatre Ensemble. Accessed June 19, 2015. "Hercules Furens." http://notmanapart.com/gallery-hercules-2013 and http://notmanapart.com/gallery-hercules [accessed 1 September 2016].

O'Kell, Eleanor Regina. 2005. *"Hercules Furens* and Nero: The Didactic Purpose of Senecan Tragedy." In Rawlings and Bowden, 185–204.

Pache, Corinne Ondine. 2004. *Baby and Child Heroes of Ancient Greece.* Urbana, IL: University of Illinois Press.

Provenza, Antonietta. 2013. "Madness and Bestialization in Euripides' *Heracles." Classical Quarterly* 63(1): 68–93.

Putnam, Michael C. J. 1995. "Virgil's Tragic Future: Senecan Drama and the *Aeneid."* In: *Virgil's Aeneid: Interpretation and Influence.* Chapel Hill, NC: University of North Carolina Press, 246–85.

Rabinowitz, Nancy Sorkin. 2014. "Women and War in Tragedy." In Meineck and Konstan, 185–206.

Rawlings, Louis. 2005. "Hannibal and Hercules." In Rawlings and Bowden, 153–84.

Rawlings, Louis, and Hugh Bowden, eds. 2005. *Herakles and Hercules: Exploring a Graeco-Roman Divinity.* Swansea: The Classical Press of Wales.

Richlin, Amy. 1992. "Reading Ovid's Rapes." In Amy Richlin, ed.. *Pornography and Representation in Greece and Rome* Oxford: Oxford University Press, 158–79.

Riley, Kathleen. 2008. *The Reception and Performance of Euripides' Herakles: Reasoning Madness.* Oxford: Oxford University Press.

Romm, James. 2014. *Dying Every Day: Seneca at the Court of Nero.* New York: Alfred A. Knopf.

Roncali, Renata. 2014. *"Apocolocyntosis."* In Damschen and Heil, 673–86.

Rosenmeyer, Thomas G. 1989. *Senecan Drama and Stoic Cosmology.* Berkeley, CA: University of California Press.

Saller, Richard P. 1994. *Patriarchy, Property, and Death in the Roman Family.* Cambridge: Cambridge University Press.

Schiesaro, Alessandro. 1997. "Passion, Reason and Knowledge in Seneca's Tragedies." In Susanna Morton Braund and Christopher Gill, eds. *The Passions in Roman Thought and Literature.* Cambridge: Cambridge University Press, 89–111.

Schlegel, August Wilhelm. 1833. *A Course of Lectures on Dramatic Art and Literature*. Tr. John Black. Philadelphia: Hogan and Thompson.

Schmidt, Ernst A. 2014. *Space and Time in Senecan Drama*. In Damschen and Heil, 531–46.

Schubert, Werner. 2014. "Seneca the Dramatist." In Damschen and Heil, 73–93.

Scodel, Ruth, ed. 1993. *Theater and Society in the Classical World*. Ann Arbor, MI: University of Michigan Press.

Shaw, Brent. 1982/3. "'Eaters of Flesh, Drinkers of Milk': The Ancient Mediterranean Ideology of the Pastoral Nomad." *Ancient Society* 13/14: 5–31.

Shay, Jonathan. 2002. *Odysseus in America: Combat Trauma and the Trials of Homecoming*. New York: Scribner.

Shay, Jonathan. 1995. *Achilles in Vietnam: Combat Trauma and the Undoing of Character*. New York: Simon & Schuster.

Shelton, Jo-Ann. 1975. "Problems of Time in Seneca's *Hercules Furens* and *Thyestes*." *California Studies in Classical Antiquity* 8: 257–69.

Shelton, Jo-Ann. 1978. *Seneca's* Hercules Furens: *Theme, Structure and Style*. Göttingen: Vandenhoeck und Ruprecht.

Sheppard, J.T. 1916. "The Formal Beauty of the *Hercules Furens*." *Classical Quarterly* 10: 72–79.

Shannon, Hannah Means. 7/17/2014. "Alan Moore Calls for Boycott of 'Wretched Film' *Hercules* on Behalf of Friend Steve Moore." http://www.bleedingcool.com/2014/07/17/alan-moore-calls-for-boycott-of-wretched-film-hercules-on-behalf-of-friend-steve-moore/ [accessed 30 August 2016].

Shirley, Don. 6/10/2013. "Adapting *Saturday Night Fever*, Shakespeare and Seneca." http://thisstage.la/2013/06/adapting-saturday-night-fever-shakespeare-and-seneca/ [accessed 30 August 2016].

Sklenár, R.J. 2003. *The Taste for Nothingness. A Study of* Virtus *and Related Themes in Lucan's* Bellum Civile. Ann Arbor, MI: University of Michigan Press.

Slaney, Helen. 2013. "Seneca's Chorus of One." In Joshua Billings, Felix Budelmann, and Fiona Macintosh, eds. *Choruses, Ancient and Modern*, 99–116.

Slaney, Helen. 2016. *The Senecan Aesthetic: A Performance History*. Oxford: Oxford University Press.

Slavitt, David R. 1992. *Seneca*. Baltimore, MD: Johns Hopkins University Press.

Soellner, Rolf. 1958. "The Madness of Hercules and the Elizabethans." *Comparative Literature* 10(4): 309–24.

Stafford, Emma. 2012. *Herakles*. New York: Routledge.

Star, Christopher. 2006. "Commanding *Constantia* in Senecan Tragedy." *Transactions of the American Philological Association* 136(1): 207–44.

Stewart, Andrew. 1993. *Faces of Power: Alexander's Image and Hellenistic Politics*. Berkeley, CA: University of California Press.

Sutton, Dana F. 1986. *Seneca on the Stage*. Leiden: E.J. Brill.

Taplin, Oliver. 2007. *Pots & Plays: Interactions between Tragedy and Greek Vase-painting of the Fourth Century B.C.* Los Angeles, CA: J. Paul Getty Museum.

Tarrant, R.J. 1978. "Senecan Drama and Its Antecedents." *Harvard Studies in Classical Philology* 82: 213–63.

Trinacty, Christopher V. 2014. *Senecan Tragedy and the Reception of Augustan Poetry*. Oxford: Oxford University Press.

Trinacty, Christopher V. 2015. "Senecan Tragedy." In Bartsch and Schiesaro, 29–40.

Trzaskoma, Stephen M., R. Scott Smith, and Stephen Brunet. 2004. *Anthology of Classical Myth*. Indianapolis: Hackett.

Wachtel, Eleanor. 2014. "Wachtel on the Arts—Peter Sellars." http://www.cbc.ca/ideas/episodes/2014/03/18/wachtel-on-the-arts---peter-sellars/ [accessed 30 August 2016].

Waith, Eugene M. 1962. *The Herculean Hero in Marlowe, Chapman, Shakespeare and Dryden*. New York: Columbia University Press.

Watling, E.F. 1966. *Seneca: Four Tragedies and Octavia*. Harmondsworth: Penguin.

Webb, Ruth. 2009. *Ekphrasis, Imagination and Persuasion in Ancient Rhetorical Theory and Practice*. Burlington, VT: Ashgate.

West, David. 1991. *Virgil: The Aeneid*. Harmondsworth: Penguin.

Williams, Gareth. 2012. *The Cosmic Viewpoint: A Study of Seneca's Natural Questions*. Oxford: Oxford University Press.

Wilson, Emily. 2010. *Seneca: Six Tragedies*. Oxford: Oxford University Press.

Wilson, Emily. 2014. *The Greatest Empire: A Life of Seneca*. Oxford: Oxford University Press.

Wiseman, T.P. 1974. "Legendary Genealogies in Late-Republican Rome." *Greece and Rome* 21: 153–64.

Wyles, Rosie. 2013. "Heracles' Costume from Euripides' *Heracles* to Pantomime Performance." In George W.M. Harrison and Vayos Liapis, eds. *Performance in Greek and Roman Theatre*. Leiden: Brill, 181–98.

Zanobi, Alessandra. 2014. *Seneca's Tragedies and the Aesthetics of Pantomime*. London: Bloomsbury.

Zeitlin, Froma I. 1986. "Thebes: Theater of Self and Society in Athenian Drama." In Peter Euben, ed. *Greek Drama and Political Theory*. Berkeley, CA: University of California Press, 101–41.

Zimmermann, Bernhard. 2008. "Seneca and Pantomime." In Edith Hall and Rosie Wyles, eds. *New Directions in Ancient Pantomime*. Oxford: Oxford University Press, 218–26.

Chronology

1997   Film *Hercules,* directed by Clements and Musker (Walt Disney
           Pictures)

1997   Video game *Disney's Hercules* (Disney Interactive)

1998–99   TV series *Disney's Hercules: The Animated Series*

2000   Video game *Hercules: The Legendary Journeys* (Titus Software)

2005   *Hercules Furens* performed in Brasenose College, Oxford, UK

2008   Five-issue comic series *Hercules: The Thracian Wars* (Moore and
           Wijaya, Radical Comics)

2014   Film *Hercules,* directed by Brett Ratner (Paramount/MGM)

Glossary of Greek and Latin Terms

alexikakos "averter of evil," a traditional cultic title of Hercules.

anapaest a meter composed of two light beats and one heavy beat, associated with marching. The first and fourth choral odes of *Hercules Furens* are composed in this meter.

Asclepiad a lyric meter used in the second choral ode of *Hercules Furens*.

aulos a flute used in the performance of classical Greek tragedy.

doubling assigning more than one role over the course of a drama to the same actor. For example, the same actor likely played both Megara and Hercules in *Hercules Furens*.

ecphrasis a description of people, places, objects, or landscape, such as Theseus' lengthy description of the Underworld in Act 3.

exostra a platform pushed out from backstage to reveal an interior scene. It is likely used in *Hercules Furens* for displaying the dead bodies of Megara and the children in Act 4.

glyconic a lyric meter used in part of the third choral ode of *Hercules Furens*.

mechane a crane used to elevate actors above the stage, often used to represent gods.

pietas the Roman sense of affective duty or obligation.

saltator a pantomime dancer.

Sapphic a lyric meter used in part of the third choral ode of *Hercules Furens*.

sententia a brief proverbial statement of traditional wisdom, such as "impetuous courage falls from a great height" (*Hercules Furens* 201).

theomachy conflict between human beings and gods, as threatened by Hercules at *Hercules Furens* 955–73.

virtus "manly spirit, resolution, valor, steadfastness" (*Oxford Latin Dictionary*).

Index

www.ingramcontent.com/pod-product-compliance
Lightning Source LLC
Chambersburg PA
CBHW070012140726
47908CB00020B/1270